Other books by Greg Dorchak:

Where Monsters Go When You Grow Up

Who Took My Crayons?!

How To Pull A Movie Out Of Your Ass

Good Shit To Know About Being A Film Actor

OF PIGS
AND
METEORITES

by G. Dorchak

Austin, Texas

Of Pigs and Meteorites

Copyright © 2024 by Greg Dorchak

Class Clown Publishing

All rights reserved.

Inquiries should be addressed to:
greg@classclownpictures.com

ISBN-13: 979-8-8689-1182-8

Library of Congress Registration Number: TX 9-349-749

Cover design by Greg Dorchak

Cover photo from author's collection

Photo on page 239 by ABM Photography

Edited by Nicole Zayas-Dorchak

Printed in the United States

A special thanks to
my mother and brother,
who helped put a finer point
on some of the lies
I've been telling myself
all these years.

For my Mother

Contents

Of Pigs and Meteorites

FOREWORD

I grew up in the northern part of the Adirondack Park, what is known as the High Peaks Region. My family moved there around 1965 when I was a little over a year old. We lived for a bit in a nice little hamlet called Cranberry Lake, while our dad attended the Ranger School in Wanakena. After that we moved to Mohawk Lake, where we stayed for awhile.

I moved away in 1979 when I was 14, and briefly moved back for about five years after I was married and had children. After moving to Austin, TX in 1991, I have been back a few times, but never lived up there again. I sometimes still miss it terribly, but I just don't think I could handle the snow and cold anymore - it's too much like work.

Though the name of the specific place I grew up, as well as the names of people I knew, have been changed to protect the privacy of those who are still alive, and the families of those who have passed on, the stories in this book are all true. Maybe slightly embellished here and there, and even a bit under-sold in other places, these are actual memories.

Memory and perspective being what they are, I can only attest that what I have written is reflective of what I recall, and how it made me feel back in the day, through the filter of time.

I hope you enjoy the stories in this book, and if you ever get the opportunity to visit the great Adirondack Park of the Empire State, do it. Just maybe not in the winter. Unless you dig that.

MEMORIES, TRIVIA AND SMARTS

Memory is a weird deal. I am not really sure what causes memories, or what makes some memories stick while others fade away, never to be heard from again; but I'll bet it has something to do with significance, trauma and interest. Plus one other thing that is like a "Double Secret Wild Card," that turns certain information into memories that stay in place for no discernible reason whatsoever. Or maybe there's a Higher Purpose and some Future Need for that information that your very life might depend on.

I also have no idea what the agreed-upon limit is on first memories, age-wise. By that I mean, in general, how far back do "first memories" tend to go for the average person. Me, I can vividly recall – still – at least three memories from being a very small child – like still in my crib small. Dear God, I hope it wasn't just my parents being cheap or poor and leaving my ass in the crib until I was seven.

I have always had a pretty good memory, and it has been both a blessing and a curse for me. Sometimes it's great remembering that kid's name from First Grade… the one who always had that green sweater on and parted his hair on the right side. Or recalling dialog from a movie from 1937, or that jingle from that commercial from 1974.

> *Hold the pickles, hold the lettuce*
> *Special orders don't upset us*
> *All we ask is that you let us serve it your way*
> *Have it YOUR way, have it your way…*

I mean, who needs to have *that* nonsense wasting space in their head 50 years later? How does that help Humanity in any way?

T*hat* bullshit, I fear, is taking up brain cells that could be better used for important information, like political or ethical shit, or life-saving first aidery. *Why* on God's Green Earth – at my age – am I remembering words, cadence and inflection for some fast food chain commercial jingle, but I can't call to mind a password I just created? What a cruel, obnoxious hoax to play on a person.

And more importantly, why am I having so much trouble learning new things? Likely because the new things can't find a purchase in my brain matter on account of all the bullshit trivia that has been lodged in there since I was two. That's what is keeping me from being smart.

By the way, there is a huge difference between being smart and knowing trivia. Being smart is figuring things out; being able to intake, parse information, and spit out a reasonable answer based on previous input and experience. Trivia is just information that doesn't matter, but like a squatter in California, it just sits around rent-free in your brain while the answer to cold fusion starves to death out on the streets.

Defending your house from invaders on Christmas Eve using odds and ends you have around the home: SMARTS. The first actor to play James Bond was Barry Nelson: TRIVIA.

I used to know so much about movies – titles, actors, lines, famous quotes, famous behind the scenes stories – just all kinds of crap. And I'm talking every time the game piece stopped on Entertainment in Trivial Pursuit, everyone else just threw their hands up and groaned because they knew that I knew that shit.

And really, the knowing of all this meaningless crap would not have been bad in and of itself – but unfortunately it was paired perfectly with my inability to keep my stupid mouth shut if I knew something. And I'm not even just talking about Trivial Pursuit either.

I was (and maybe still am) pretty much medically unable to not blurt things out if I knew them – it really wasn't that I was trying to show how smart I was – because we have established that trivia is not smarts.

I simply could not pass up an opportunity to blurt out information when a moment arrived where there was pertinent information in my head that shed light on a matter at hand.

Such as when friends and family were watching a movie, and I had seen it before, and this was that scene where that thing happens, and I just *knew* no one else knew it. Or when everyone in a room saw a bird at the window, and it became pretty evident that absolutely no one but myself knew the etymology of the bird's name and what sort of digestive tract they had.

Quite frankly, it was exhausting being the Prometheus, Bringer of Fire. I cared too much, I think was the problem.

But as I have gotten older, the memory thing merely frightens me... on a good day. I have reached the age where I finally know why experts say memory is an unreliable witness, and now, many times, I am able to just shut my yapper before it fires up. Unreliable. I used to know with certainty that when I remembered something, by God *that* memory was 100 percent factual. I *know* I looked at that thermometer on that particular day, and it WAS indeed 47 degrees below outside, because it was that brand new thermometer we bought at Home Depot when we lived in that house in Mohawk Lake.

Only, the Internet now says that it never got that cold in the entire year in that part of New York State; and Home Depot wasn't established there until years later. So what the hell were those memories?

Lousy Internet.

It erases our memories and makes shit up to replace them. And even on its best day, the internet usually winds up simply being complicit in the lies we try to tell ourselves about what it is we know. When someone hears something that disagrees with their own belief, the offended person usually only looks up *their* side of the story, and stops when they find the thing that agrees with their knowledge. But they never look up the other side.

Let's take a For Instance. Recently, I was sitting in the room when these two young people (early 20s) were talking about eating a turkey sandwich for lunch. One person said they were going to have a turkey sandwich for lunch. The other person said no, they were not, because they didn't want to fall asleep immediately after lunch.

"Pardon me?" was the reply, "fall asleep?"

"Yes," said the non-turkey-sandwich-eater. "Turkey has tryptophan in it, and tryptophan makes you fall asleep."

"The devil, you say!"

"It is, indeed, facts."

Turkey-sandwich-eater scoffed; maybe even hawed or hemmed, still not sold on the subject. At which point, non-turkey-sandwich-eater turned to me – because I may have looked like someone who knew a thing or two – and said:

"Isn't that right, Greg, turkey makes you fall asleep because tryptophan?"

AHA! The incantation had been spake, The Knowing had been summoned!

"Actually," I said in a matter-o-factly way, "That was a pretty commonly accepted misconception. Studies have since shown that people typically get sleepy at Thanksgiving not because of the turkey, but because they usually ingest a large amount of carbs with it, and the carbs are mostly responsible for the sleepiness. Moreover..."

Non-Turkey-Sandwich-Eater did not even blink, they picked up their phone – as is an young person's wont – and did an internet search.

"Yep," they announced triumphantly, and in total oblivion to anything I may have said, "Turkey has tryptophan in it."

And then, pleased with the results that matched their thought, the dialogue continued, no pauses taken, no second turkey sandwich made.

Here's the thing: we were both correct. I just happened to be more correct for the discussion's point. YES, turkey has tryptophan in it. And, yes, tryptophan makes you sleepy. However, because of the amount of turkey you'd have to ingest to create the sleepy-feeling, it had been determined by Dr. Jeffrey Science, that it was the large amounts of carbohydrates that were consumed with the turkey that made folks sleepy. One would have to eat about ten pounds of ONLY turkey to drift off to Slumberland; certainly not three slices of Hillshire Farms sandwich-thickness oven-roasted sliced turkey. You'd actually get more sleepy from a glass of milk than a turkey sandwich.

I knew this. I am no science person, but I knew this because at some point in my life I read it or heard it from a reliable source, and my brain deemed it fit to be forever engraved on a synapse for easy retrieval. *This*, is indeed *facts*.

So, I have my earliest memories, and no one can say they are not real and true, because I still see them like they were yesterday, even here on the back nine of the golf course of my life. There is no internet to check on it, but I don't need it. I was there, I saw these things. Just like I know I was young, because I was still in my crib when I watched as my father, grandfather and neighbor installed the new baseboard-mounted radiator rails in what would later become my oldest brother's room. In my crib still, sooooo, what... two years old *at most*. Right?

I also recall crying loudly while lying on my back as I watched a huge spider slowly, haltingly, descend from a thread over my crib, and my mother came in and grabbed the spider by the web and took it to flush it down the toilet. So, likely still a baby there too.

With 600dpi clarity, I saw that shadow, shaped like a spy in a trench coat slinking about my room, trying to get closer to my crib so it could snatch me away, until my mother came in and turned on the light, forcing that sneaky beggar to dodge behind the dresser against the wall, never to be seen again.*

---

* I will concede here, because I know I was a baby in a crib, these last two memories could likely have occurred in either Whitefield, New Hampshire, or Cranberry Lake, New York, or any combination of the two.

Were any of these the most significant parts of my very new childhood? Was I really just totes into the activities I was engaged in? Was this the worst shit that ever happened to me? What future calamity awaited me down the road that made it imperative that I recall them in ridiculous detail 56 years later on?

I mean, it sure as hell ain't trivia, because I am reasonably certain that there is ever going to be a Trivial Pursuit upgrade version that has questions about me or my earliest memories. And the stories aren't anything my friends can fact-check at the bar in order to see if they have to buy the next round. Yet those memories stick there *hard*, like the Burger King jingle, or Barry Nelson, or turkey-tiredness. Oddly enough, at the age I am now – that kind of bothers me a bit.

Do I want answers? Maybe, maybe not. Very likely, at my age, I would just forget the answers by the next time it came around to nagging at me again, so why bother. And besides, that's what the internet is for.

WTF IS A HAMLET?

There is a hierarchy to civilizations, like the actual communities where folks live. The city, town or whatever. It goes something like this, in descending order, according to population, courtesy of Dr. Shirley Internet:

Gigalopolis - a group of megalopolises, typically over one hundred million residents

Megalopolis - supercity of conurbations, typically over ten million residents in total

Conurbation - a group of metropolises, between three and ten million residents

Metropolis - large city with multiple satellite cities and towns. One to three million

City - large population and many services. Around one million people

Town - low density: 1,000 to 100,000 residents

Village - larger than a hamlet, smaller than a town. An average population in the hundreds

Hamlet - tiny population (couple hundred), very few buildings, no main town hall

The only thing smaller than a Hamlet is a Homestead, which usually consists of a cluster of isolated dwellings normally occupied by a single, extended family; often considered to be the smallest type of human settlement. After that, you camping in a pup-tent or under a log on your own.

Where I grew up, out in the BFE of the northern Adirondack Park, the population was low. "Pop. 500," according to the official green sign that announced one's entry to the area. I knew it wasn't a city, because my cousins and grandparents lived down in The City, and we visited, and there was a very stark contrast between where we lived, and Yonkers.

I guess I never really thought about it as a boy, but I never really knew what the designation was for our community. Fairly close by us was The Village of Saranac Lake, and a suburb(?) of it called the Town of Harrietstown, which clearly were a village or town of some sort, because they had "village" or "town" right there in the name. Down the road from us was Mohawk Lake Junction, which started out as a sort of crossroads where the train stopped back in the 1800s. But what was a "Junction," whatever *that* was, and so then what were we called if we were a "suburb" of the "Junction?" I have seen Mohawk Lake listed as a hamlet in various places, but the definition of a hamlet can vary from definition to definition. It seems close enough, so let's call it that.

I knew there were not a lot of people, that was for sure. Neighbors typically had quite a bit of room between their houses, and almost all the plots of land were measured in acreage, not square feet. And when you drove through, after passing the "hello" sign, if you blinked you'd miss the "goodbye" sign.

We lived nearly on the lake that our area was named after. You had to cross the road, and then walk a few hundred feet, and then boom, lake front. The view from the house was fantastic. The road was a little two-lane country road, it was paved, and when they put actual street lights in at some point in the early 70s, yes, we stayed out some nights to watch them come on; and, yes, it was the most amazing thing ever.

Everybody knew where everybody else lived, and I am reasonably sure there were no actual address numbers on any house. If anyone ever asked for an address, the answer was something like: "over by that huge stump close to the pond," or "just before you hit the train tracks, there's that road, make a right," or "they live in the old Hudak house."

I didn't get a lot of mail when I was a kid, but whenever I had the occasion to get something mailed to me it, like if I ordered a Halloween mask that was a "lifelike" rubber reproduction of the Creature from the Black Lagoon's face, the address was just:

Greg Dorchak

Mohawk Lake, NY 12345

That was it.

There was no apartment number, no building number, no C/o, no third or even fourth line in there at all like I had seen on some addresses I had mailed things to. I once asked my mother how long an address had to be, and she responded something like "Long enough to get the letter where it needs to go." So I was okay with that.

The original Post Office building was built maybe around 1906, and it would be almost 80 years before the new "modern" post office was built, sitting not far from the original location today.

It serves the roughly 500 residents between Mohawk Lake and Mohawk Lake Junction – so basically the "Greater Mohawk Lake Metropolitan area" – give or take. There were likely a lot fewer residents back in the day, since when I saw that "pop. 500" it was years later when I was an adult and I drove back through that area. Twenty something years after I lived there, and that number included the Junction. 500.

I recently looked up the official population of *just* Mohawk Lake... it was in the upper 300s. (Side note: Cranberry Lake, where we lived right before we moved to the thriving metropolis of Mohawk Lake, had – as of 2023 – a population of about 136.)

Sooooo... *sparse*. Yet we had every type of person in that settlement, whatever it was. We had the smart folks, the dumb folks, the helpers and the bullies, the fortunate and the un, the assholes and the nice people. You'll notice I said nothing about the drunks, but that's only because that was a baseline, I think, for that whole region in general. Everybody drank. Not necessarily to excess, and certainly nobody was going to call anyone else a drunk for having a bit too much that One Time, because that opened the door to getting called a drunk themselves the next weekend.

My dad's watering hole of choice was a little tavern in Mohawk Lake Junction, kind of behind where the old post office was, named Connor's Inn. It felt more like a totally tricked-out basement in a private home than an actual bar. It started out as a whistle-stop joint for folks coming in on the train from Malone or Lake Placid. When the trains stopped coming, it just continued being a little one-room place with a pool table taking up most of that room.

Regulars filled the chairs at the few small tables, and some barstools bathed in the yellow glow of the few requisite bar signs on the wall above the hooch. "Molson," they proclaimed, or "Labatt's," they suggested. I went there once or twice with Dad, sat there quietly sipping a White Rock soda while he had a beer with his friends.

I recently looked them up again – Connor's. They are a lot bigger now, and it's actually a campground. Winter and summer use; you can rent canoes or snowmobiles to drive after you drink your Labatts Blue or Old Milwaukee. There are even some cabins now, I think, that face out onto Mohawk Lake itself. Pretty nice setup. Way to go Connor, if you still own it.

Believe it or not, there was also an airport in Mohawk Lake. A little regional landing strip type thing – but even it has been upgraded to be able to handle some bigger planes now. I think the 1980 Olympics may have had something to do with that. There was a trailer park right by the airport as well; my two oldest and best friends (back then) lived at that park when I met them.

I don't recall having any pre-conceived notions about what it meant to live in a trailer park when I was a kid; it was just where my friends lived. And my mom, who was a Registered Nurse, used to visit folks there to make sure they were okay.

All of this was a quick, fun three-to-five-mile-ish bike ride for me, most of it a straight, flat line, where a kid on a one-speed banana-seated bike could just really let go and peddle like the freakin' wind on a summer day.

Bob's Store was across the road from the trailer park, a one room building with twelve-year old Twinkies and sodas available. I'm not even sure that was the real name of the store, everyone just called it that, perhaps, because the guy who owned it was named Bob. One gas pump, and I remember the lines at that one pump during the Energy Crisis of the 70's. We had to get in line on certain days to get our tank of gas at the greatly inflated cost of 75 cents a gallon.

The type of bullies in this community were pretty standard; shove you around, take your lunch money, call you some pretty clever names that either rhymed with your first or last name, or a particular feature of your body. They'd do this with little provocation, and with less remorse.

Fight back, and chances were one of two things might happen: you'd have a new best friend, or twice as many would now come after you. Look at them wrong... get in a fight. Say absolutely nothing, and then deny it when asked... get in a fight. Have your older sibling intervene... get in a fight. Have *their* older sibling, especially a sister, intervene... oh they'd get you for that, it'd just take a bit more time... but they'd get you, man.

Sometimes the kids weren't bullies, they just played rougher than I did. I mean, it really was a rough place to live when all was said and done. And some of these kids (and adults) were literally descendants of the first people to settle the area. So, I mean, what do you expect? Great Grampaw fought grizzly bears and the rapids, the natural progression from that activity is taking the eleven cents I brought for a half pint of milk at lunchtime.

It was always fun when I was able to see them rough kids taken down a notch or two. This one Halloween, I was down at a party at the Catholic church just down the road from us, two of these local kids, a few years older than me, came in and sat down flanking me. We definitely were not playground buddies, but they slid up to me, their candy sacks in their laps. One of them huffed "What is your brother wearing this year?"

"A Death costume," I said flatly, "why?"

"FUUUUUUUCK. He just scared the living *shit* out of us," one stated.

This wasn't in a frightened tone, or even a "we are about to mess you up for what he did" tone; but almost a tone of awe or respect.

Turns out, they were going up and down the street doing whatever it is rough kids do, smashing jack-o-lanterns, filling mail boxes with Barbasol, taking more than one piece of candy from an Honor System Bowl, and what not. As they were running from the great fun they had at a neighbor's house, they were looking back and laughing as they ran, and then they turned in the direction they were running.

Out of the tree line stepped my almost six foot tall brother in his work boots and a dark poncho with a full-head skull mask on, and holding a big-assed REAL scythe in one hand (we had those lying around our house, or rather barn). My brother just stepped in front of them and stopped. They stopped. They took one glance at him, then turned around and ran the other direction. They didn't stop till they got to the church and sat next to me.

Other than *that* sort of shenanigans, I'd say folks were pretty "normal" – but not the sort of normal you always see in the Hallmark Christmas Special type of movies. But the normal you'd see in a horror movie, where if anyone moved into town the locals would be suspicious and nosey. And if the new person were someone who had left a long time ago, and was just now coming back after so many years, they'd probably be seen some hoity-toity City Person. Conversely, that little town or hamlet would hold some charm for about three days before the city person started climbing the walls looking for "something fun to do."

Well, as fate would have it, I was that person – the one who grew up there, but moved away for a bit, and then returned. Got to tell you, the movies get that part right, it was a weird feeling being back, and I never felt like I fit in again. For the record, I never felt that I fit in when I lived there as a kid either, but it was more palpable as an adult. There were a few of my old friends I met who remembered me, and we got along okay, but it just never gelled. I was an outsider, or at best a sort of novelty or curiosity. I just felt like a normal person, but not to the Lifers.

If there was some local, who was born and raised in that little town and never left for any length of time, they would have had to do a lot, and I mean a LOT, to be side-eyed, ostracized, or cast out. When I moved back in my mid 20s, I met this guy who was maybe ten years or more older than me; and I will not mince words, he was pretty dense. If anyone had met him that was not from that area, they would have thought he had dropped out of school around 3rd grade and landed on his head wrong.

He couldn't do anything right, he was lazy and stupid and just not a very nice person. But all his friends just laughed and waved it off – "Oh, that's just ol' Mike (not his real name)," they'd explain. He'd screw up some simple job they'd give him, then he'd spend fifteen hours of their precious life-time explaining what exactly went wrong, and why and how it wasn't his fault. And then he'd move on to the next project, certain to provide the same level of work. Unbelievable. I don't know, or maybe very believable.

Going back to where I grew up was also a pretty good life-lesson teacher. This rather ordinary guy came into the place I worked one day, and he placed an order. I took down the order, then proceeded to get his contact info. He said his name, and I paused for the very slightest of seconds, then tilted my head up and looked him in the eye.

He was more than ten or fifteen years older than the last time I saw him, and he looked a bit haggard for that short amount of time, almost a defeated look on his face. But there was no doubt, it was him – one of my long-time bullies from my past. The tough, assholey look was no longer there, and what really got me was the fact that he was actually kind of small – shorter than me, and I ain't that tall. I think he reached his full height by grade five and just never grew any more.

My very first reaction was, obviously, to twist his arm, shove him against the counter and demand his lunch money; but that felt rather pedestrian. I finished taking his order, and he left. I wasn't there when he came in to get his order a few days later, and I never saw him again; but if I had thought much about the whole thing, it was enough that I saw him for what he was, just another person with fears and anxiety, that for a brief moment in time was relieved by dumping it on someone else.

Now he was just like the rest of us, trying to get through life, paying the bills, navigating the relationships, stuck in that tiny little town, or village or hamlet, or whatever the hell it was, likely unable to break free from that mold he made for himself when he was younger and didn't know anything. I think I actually felt sorry for him at one point.

The only big difference between him and me was the fact that I had moved away for a while, and indeed I would never move back to that area again. The area had not changed at all, for all intents and purposes, but the people sort of had. More likely, it was me that changed. Even in my limited exposure to Others out there in The World, I had seen what was available and what was possible – and this little community was no longer something I felt particularly connected to.

But as a kid, back in the 60s and 70s – that little hamlet out in the BFE of the Adirondack Park was the best place on Earth to grow up, and I'm glad I spent the time there.

A CHICKEN WITH ITS HEAD CUT OFF

Life is different when you have to raise your own food, be it plants or animals. And that difference takes on yet another interesting layer when it is also up to you to process that food, be it plants or animals. On our little subsistence farm, we had to grow enough vegetables and fruits, chickens, turkeys and pigs to last a family of between six or eight for a long winter.

On any given year we had about two or three dozen layers – that is chickens that were for eggs, not eating; and about another 100 of eatin' chickens; a dozen turkeys, two or three pigs, and a few acres of beans, peas, carrots, squash, corn, peppers, melons, wild blueberries and strawberries, apples, rhubarb and crabapples and whatever else our dad found for us to go pick on a roadside.

I want to start out by saying I understand the argument on both sides of eating animals, and I happen to fall on the side of eating animals. I respect my friends, and anyone really, who is on the side of not. I get it and I get the reasons, and so I will try to be cognizant of these folks when I describe how my childhood taught me to live and work with animals that were not pets.

PSA here: do not name your dinner.

However tasty I think animals are, and whatever benefits there are from consuming them, I am not in favor of the bullshit that gets done in the name of the fine dinings, and the haute cuisines, and especially not those weird a-holes that go to great lengths to make dining some sort of participatory performance art event where unsuspecting diners try in vain to take a bite out of a cloud of gas served over a bed of deconstructed toast points.

I have never even entertained the idea of becoming a vegetarian or vegan, I try to eat a healthy balance of vegetation and meat. In my head, everything eats something else to survive in this world, it's the way it is set up; so I see no logical reason why humans should have been the only creature on earth that was "not meant to eat meat." Just don't be a dick about it, I say. Though I also think that if everyone were to become vegans, perhaps we'd all be too weak and malnourished to start or prolong wars and physical violence against each other.

Where I come from, you eat animals and plants to survive, and you respect and take care of those animals and plants, because without them you die a long and particularly uncomfortable death. I have never liked veal, the thought of it makes me want to practice the same method on the humans who came up with it. Stupid shit like that, just to get a tastier piece of meat, I am not jake with. I also am not okay with wasting food. To this day, sometimes even when it ain't good for me, I tend to try to finish everything on my plate.

I am not a picky eater. Those who know me, and have been at the table in restaurants when it happens, know I will eat what I am brought – even when I ordered enchiladas with charro beans but I get grilled tilapia with the roasted vegetable melody – I just eat it.

"But that's not what you ordered… send it back," my friends will say.

"It's food," I'll say. "Likely they'll just throw it away if I send it back, or the chef will poison the next plate, or I may even get something even weirder."

I'll just eat it, it's food. But it is pretty comical, the frequency with which this happens, and it's kind of like a lottery or a chance to lay bets on what I actually will get whenever we go out to eat.

We were out with a friend once, in his town, and he took us to one of his favorite burger joints. Somehow the subject came up about not getting what you ordered, and my friend just kind of laughed it off. My wife and I shot each other a knowing glance and said nothing else. We all ordered some tasty-sounding burgers, and ordered some local beers and ciders while we waited.

It wasn't long before the waiter came back looking sheepish – she walked right up to me.

"I'm sorry," she explained, "But we don't have any more of X Cider."

My friend raised an eyebrow. I ordered something else.

Five minutes later the waiter came back again.

"I..." she started.

"You are out of it." I stated.

"Yes." She apologized.

"Okay, let's make this easy, just bring me whatever kind of cider you do have," I said. "And if you have zero ciders left, surprise me with a local beer."

She left. My friend looked at me and laughed. My wife said something like "I bet you thought we were exaggerating, huh?"

"Well, at least you'll get a cider," my friend said.

The waiter returned with my Surprise Local Beer.

My friend laughed, and was not quite done laughing when the servers arrived with our meals. They set the tasty burgers in front of my wife and friend, and then set a grilled chicken sandwich in front of me. We had all ordered burgers. It was very specifically a place known for its burgers. My wife and I stated that we were first-timers and wanted to try their legendary local masterpiece burger. I didn't even blink.

"Boom." I said. My friend was dumbstruck. We ate. It was just another day for me.

When I was maybe seven or eight, I heard the shout for dinner from the house, but I was having too much fun doing whatever I was doing down by the lake. I didn't even shout back. We were always told: get to dinner on time, or you get what you get. On this night, I got to the table fifteen or twenty minutes late, and was barely able to serve myself one slightly-heaping serving spoon of mashed potatoes. And that was it.

I saw the steak bones, and the stripped corn cobs, so I knew that food was there at one point. And knowing my oldest brother, I was *certain* that bastard ate my steak, and most definitely laughed while he did so. But no, I got a spoonful of starch, and was stuck with that.

Was I ever late to dinner again? No.

Our fall months were one long day, filled with cutting and stacking firewood, picking and canning or freezing veggies and fruit, and… getting those animals into and edible form. The pigs were very easy, they got sent out, we did not have the facilities to process them correctly and quickly. But the chickens and turkeys… they done learnt, and they done learnt TODAY.

Turkeys were a tad tougher than chickens, we had to take them out with a .22 before plucking and gutting and chopping and packing. The chickens, well you may have seen some movies or shows where small farm folks would "ring their necks" – which was pretty much what is sounds like – to make a chicken more amenable to not being alive. We didn't do that, we were civilized. We had axes.

Our chicken coop – for the eaters – was a single box pen up on stilts sitting about two feet off the ground. A wooden framed box with a shelter on one end for the chickens to get out of the rain, and the other end was all just chicken wire so they could run around pooping to their hearts' content, which would just fertilize the wild strawberries growing underneath the coop.

Turkeys had the same, though as I found out, turkeys are rather dumb. They would often not use the shelter and just stand there, staring up at the rain, sometimes even to the point where they would drown as their mouths collected enough water to choke on. That's if they were lucky enough to not get pecked to death by their roommates because their wattle looked like something they could peck at and eat.

There were one or two occasions where I had come home from school, went to water the turkeys, and found one of them bloodied and dead on the floor of the cage. I checked for holes in the cage to see if something had gotten in, did a remaining head count and found them all accounted for. Later my dad would tell me how turkeys pretty much go full Lord of the Flies when no one is looking. It ain't pretty.

Becoming dinner is the best thing that can happen to a turkey, they should welcome it over rain-drowning or friend-pecking any day of the year. The peace that came with being prepped to feed a family should have been looked forward to; and for all I know, maybe it was.

But really, our poultry lived a rather simple life, with room to run around, fresh grass and bugs to eat, two main meals per day of whatever makes up poultry food, and unlimited fresh air. Spring and summer passed like a dream.

Then one day it was Fall, and things changed.

(NOTE: I am about to explain something here that may be a bit on the graphic side. This is not for the faint of heart, so I will try to tone it down best I can, omitting some of the gorier details where I can. I will give you a moment to get the appropriate folks out of the room before I continue.)

In the fall, someone had to climb into the pen and grab all the chickens, one by one, and hand them out to my father or grandfather, who would then (details omitted) and then hand the now-still body to the other person who would stack them in the trusty little blue metal Ford wagon for transport.

People may occasionally think about chickens getting (details omitted), but I'm not sure they think about it very deeply. Chicken is HERE, it gets chaperoned over to THERE, then they (details omitted), and the body goes in a wagon.

But the fact is that, in a fixed environment, where the other chickens are all pretty much sitting *right there*, a realization occurs after seeing one after another of your roommates all get (details omitted) seven feet away.

First chicken: okay, wow, *that* happened; sorry to see you go Tony. Second chicken: oh, DAMN, okay… third fourth fifth chicken… as dumb as the average chicken is, well, they notice a pattern at some point.

Then there is that Last Chicken.

Now that Last Chicken… that is what we call – in farm lingo – a highly motivated chicken. That chicken is deeply engaged in a protocol known as "AWWW HELLLLLL NO."

I was pretty small when I was a kid, but I still had to squat-walk in that cage to grab the chickens. By that Last Chicken, I am certain that there was more than one person behind me chuckling a bit much as they watched me squat-sprint after that last, highly-motivated chicken. And I actually thank whatever force there is out there that the invention of cell phones with cameras was still more than twenty years off.

Well, as it happened, that Last Chicken finally got to participate in (details omission). It was inevitable. Perhaps to commemorate the event, or perhaps just in a moment of Hemmingwayian enlightenment on how to make me into a man, Dad decided that instead of handing me the chicken's still body to place in the wagon, he was just gonna (details omit) it, and *immediately* toss the body at me.

I went to catch it, because what did I know, but it went right between my hands, and hit me square in the chest. Then this chicken with its (details) *very* recently (omitted) began to flap WAY more than I ever saw a live one flap, and spurted (details) all over the place (the "place" being "me') via the (detail) in its (omitted). The flapping subsided quickly, and in a cloud of feathers it dropped to the ground, where it… well, ran around like a chicken with its head cut off.

So now I had to chase it once more, getting slightly less motivated with each step (that would refer to both me and the chicken). It is worth noting here that there is a certain amount of shame attached to losing a foot race with a headless chicken.

I finally tracked it down under a bush, and finished its trip to the wagon, where I set it down among the other. I looked down at my clothes and hands – I now sported a really large Red Badge of Courage on my T-shirt, and my hands had (details) all over them. I listened to the laughter all in good fun from the adults around me. It was indeed the best of times and the worst of times.

The wagon would get pulled by the little Ford tractor down to the barn, where stations would be set up to (details omitted) and wrap the prepped food, then it would immediately be jammed into one of the three or four freezers we had on our back porch.

These were farm-grown animals, by the way – fresh air, healthy-ish food, bug and grass supplements, no weird steroids or drugs; so our regular chickens were the size of small turkeys, and our turkeys were the size of large turkeys. We had 30+ pound gobblers for Thanksgiving and Christmas, and an assortment of other days.

The processing area, which started outside the barn, was an education in itself. The rope line that went from a birch tree to the corner of the barn, held the load of current participants, each (details omitted), until we could dunk them, one by one first into hot water, then into cold water, and then back and forth for a bit to help loosen the hold they had on their feathers.

We would then pluck them down until they more closely resembled what you buy in the Grand Union or A & P, and then we'd bring them inside to Margo, our neighbor. Margo was in charge of taking what was inside a chicken, and guiding it to the outside of the chicken. She was perfectly suited to this work because she worked in the morgue at the local hospital. What was always kind of amusing to me, especially in hindsight, was the fact that Margo used a scalpel and was meticulous in her work, when really all she had needed to do was take a sharp kitchen knife and (details omitted).

But she took pride in her work, and often stopped to show me the different things you could find on the inside of a chicken, such as (omitted), a couple (omitted), and the usual (omitted), (omitted), and (omitted). And sometimes eggs.

Fortunately, the animal processing usually only took the weekend to finish, a couple really long days, so it was over quickly. I truly cannot say whether or not I had any feelings attached to the work – such as I "enjoyed" it or "dreaded" it. It was simply work that needed doing, and you did it.

So whether or not we cared for the messy wet-work, when we had food all winter – we did enjoy that. And I will admit, any time I have heard the phase "running around like a chicken with its head cut off," tossed around flippantly, I have also enjoyed going into detail describing what it actually looks like to some Normie. And if that description were to interrupt their meal of basswood-braised veal nodules in a clam-reduction over sustainable gluten-free, setting-3.5-toasted toast points... all the better.

STOICISM FOR FUN AND PROFIT

I have never been accused of being overly-emotional. That is, of course, unless you count anger as an emotion; but who does that, amiright? Oh, and maybe crying after I had been angered at, so there's that. But crying isn't an emotion either, so there you have it.

My family was not big on emotions, so there was not really a vast modeling pool to draw from. When I got older, I understood the whys of it, I mean the place and time that both sets of parents came from, and more importantly, where *their* parents came from – *that* gene pool was to blame, or thank.

Both sets of grandparents – and mind you, these were all working-class children of immigrants and actual immigrants, not wealthy or even well-to-do – wherever they came from, were the generation to live through the Flu Pandemic of 1917-18, the Great Depression *and* World Wars I & II; if *those* didn't numb the living shit out of one's emotional pool, I don't know what would.

And *their* parents, hell, they were the ones who had to cram into ships' holds and splash across the Atlantic to the US and work in crappy conditions, cramped into tenement houses in one of the biggest cities in the country. *Their* parents, likely had it cushy over in Old Countria, where they had lived forever in dreamlike splendor, picking beets, hammering iron into steel, fixing wagons, and trying not to die of The Plague. Hmmm, it begins to show a bit of a pattern. Where, exactly was I supposed to get emotions from? Where the hell was *anyone* supposed to get emotions from with relatives like that?

Anyway, there were days when I felt my inability to feel – or perhaps, rather, to express – emotions other than anger might have been beneficial to me. Taking a pounding from a bully, obvs. If a bully didn't see you cry, that really kind of whipped some of the fun out of that transaction for them. By extension, this same principle worked with general physical injuries as well, by not making them worse in a psychological way.

Say you stabbed yourself with a mis-handled screwdriver or knife, or dropped a brick on your foot in your haste to finish a chore quickly in order to not miss the Bugs Bunny Road Runner Show on Saturday morning. Getting upset always just seemed to make the matter worse. There was *always* some injury on a farm, either from work or from play. Emotions would lengthen the time it took to get back to "normal." So why bother?

Injury, immediately followed by cleaning the wound if needed, applying a band-aid, or perhaps a trip to the ER... total time spent maybe two hours at most; 5 minutes on the DIY low end, sans-ER.

But injury, immediately followed by crying and whining and flailing about, then parental intervention that could involve anything from attempts at calming you down, to trying to force you to shut up and get back to work, or an added injury from the punishment you got at breaking the thing that injured you to begin with, was now a consideration. Add to that any additional stress from the look on the parent's face upon seeing the injury, noticing that it was either severe enough for the ER, or perhaps so severe that you might as well dig your own shallow grave out back, well, that just took too much time to make it worth the effort.

So a monthly subscription to Stoicism+ it was then. The "plus" being anger. And we were Vikings at it.

Having this gene in my own personal pool, I realize now I could have parlayed such behavior into a cash business, had I only realized it years earlier. I really missed out on a great opportunity. Not from the anger aspect, but from the un-flappability thing, the stoicism gene.

I had heard stories from my paternal grandparents for years when I was young. They would both tell me their own stories about my grandmother's family that owned a funeral home in Yonkers, that Grandma's brother married into, and now ran with his wife, who back in the day, was the youngest woman to receive a funeral director's license in the City of Yonkers.

I was maybe 10 or 11, when Grandpa would tell me the story about how he found out that a friend of his had passed away. One day (this is when my grandfather was maybe in his 30s), while visiting his brother-in-law Bill at the funeral home, Bill asked him to please go down to the basement and bring up this item that Bill needed. Grandpa, being affable, went down the stairs, and was reaching out for the light's pull cord that always seemed to be a thing in basements and cellars, when his hand landed on something cold and clammy.

Grandpa waved his hand away (I mean he knew what it was), found the light cord, and pulled it. There on a table in front of him, was the body of his friend – good lord I hoped it was only a passing acquaintance, but I swear he kept saying "a friend" – ready for Funeral Homenning. And he LAUGHED when he told this story. Bill and he laughed at the time. Seriously? "Oh, you got me, I thought Ted was still alive, and here he is dead on a stainless steel table!"

This was what passed for a practical joke in my family tree. Exhibit A.

I know I would have made a great funeral home worker, and likely could have made a life-long career out of it. Probably one of the most secure gigs there is, incidentally. Hindsight.

There were some fun aspects of this gene as well; times when the anger, in grudge form, truly made me smile, even if the extenuating circumstances should have mitigated that fun. When my paternal grandmother was very ill toward the end of her corporeal days, there was what we now refer to as The Scrap Book Maneuver.

Grandma was home for a bit, after she had gotten out of the hospital for some Cancer and Diabetes-related issues. She was not in great shape, almost 80, using a walker, post-chemo and whatnot. We were sitting at the kitchen table, my grandparents and my wife and I, looking through their old scrap books. The pictures in this one book were from the 30s and 40's – we were currently in the late 80's – so at least 50-60 years had passed since these photos were taken.

At one point, my dear, frail, old grandmother turned a yellowed page full of scallop-edged sepia-toned photos, and before any of us could even blink, she had peeled up the cellophane page-protector, whipped out one of the photos from the page, and tore it to pieces right in front of us, and chucked it in the trash. She then proceeded to trash-talk the woman in the picture with much vigor. Her facial expression never changed, her voice was even and emotionless, like some sort of Russian Hannahbelle Lecter.

We just sat there and waited patiently as Grandma got up, announced she was tired and was now going to take a nap, and watched as Grandpa helped her to their room.

We did the only thing we could, and what adult protocol dictated: we quietly scampered to the trash, snatched all the torn picture scraps from the can, and went to the living room to piece them together. The person in the picture, a fairly handsome, nicely-dressed woman in a long winter coat standing next to a Pierce Arrow (that's a car) was not of particular interest. What was of particular interest, especially to my wife, was the text on the back of the old photo:

Jane Policheck
Saratoga Springs – 1936

1936. Roughly 52 years earlier. Grandma had managed to keep a grudge roiling in her head for 52 years. This grudge was so intact, that she was able, even in her diminished physical state, to move with superhuman speed to erase this woman's image before any of us knew what had happened. I was in awe. I mean, I knew I could hold a grudge, I was holding a few at the time of this event, but the three grudges I had working together didn't even add up to 52-year's-worth of time. THIS? This was like me being wronged by someone at age 4 and still being pissed as of this book's writing. Grandma was my personal hero.

My wife, she just looked at me with what seemed to be new eyes, and said "FUCK. That explains a lot." She had *no* idea. Well, I guess *now* she had. Literally. That maneuver amazes me to this day.

I know you are dying to know the backstory on that Jane Policheck lady, and frankly, so was I. I got an answer a tiny bit later. On a rainy afternoon, I stayed home with Grandma to watch her soaps and work on crossword puzzles with her, instead of going off to help Grandpa at Dad's place. The fact that Grandpa still went even though it was raining pretty good, got Grandma into a bit of a mood, which she chatted about as we watched Days of Our Lives.

"He always just does what he wants," she spat. And I mean literally spat. Grandma used to spit into a tissue that she kept tucked up under her left sleeve, specifically for times such as these. Especially if she were not close to the kitchen sink. "I should have married that nice Protestant fellah when I had the chance."

I raised my eyebrows, turned the volume on the TV down a bit, and looked away from the drama involving whomever was cheating on whom, and looked at Grandma... gotta tell you, I was keen to know. Thank God my stoic nature was able to mask my giddiness at the prospect of hearing some really old family gossip – especially about this situation.

Without any further provocation, as if I wasn't even in the room, she spat out phrases here and there that, when pieced together, created a patchwork quilt of the early years of her relationship with Grandpa.

Apparently, the two had had a fight, involving that time her no-good (circa 1936) fiancee (Grandpa) had gone for a little ride in his car (Pierce Arrow) with a "friend" named Jane (Policheck) out to some place (Saratoga Springs). LADY JANE, as Grandma called her, NOT in an endearing way. The fight was so formidable, that they had split up for a short while, during which time Grandma had met "this nice Protestant fellah" who had proposed to her as well.

I honestly could not tell what the modifier "Protestant" was supposed to mean. Was it just a common adjectival practice used to separate this gentleman from all the other Baptists, engineers, and fish mongers? Or was it meant to be a nasty jab at Grandpa a la "Oh sure, you're *Catholic*... but this guy is even better than you, and he's a *Protestant*?" Oh, daaaaammmmnnnn, take

THAT Grandpa. I mean, of all the things she could have said that qualified this other guy – who, sadly, she never named – the best one she had in her head all these years was Protestant. Not even "This handsomer young stud," or "That jaunty French shoe salesman,"or the simpler "The man I really loved."

Well, it really didn't matter much, because as relationships do, Grandma and Grandpa eventually made up, and of course got married, and everything was Jake from then on. Grandma cussed and growled for a bit, until the drama on the TV sucked her in again, and she eventually even forgot about Grandpa going off to work in the rain. Except no, she didn't.

When he returned home some hours later, Grandma jumped up, had some choice words for him, mixing the two times (1936 and "now"), and then stomped (as well as she could, with a walker) away into the kitchen to make dinner. Grandpa sighed, took off his hat and coat, and uttered one of his favorite catch phrases as he hung his things up:

"Well, Greg... what're ya gonna do?" he sighed, and went in to help Grandma with dinner.

And that phrase, right there: "What're ya gonna do?" THAT describes the nuance and attraction to the state of Stoicism TO A TEE. What, indeed, *are* you gonna do? Can you fix the situation with emotion? Would it help in any way if you had a fit, started to scream and flail your arms about?

"What're ya gonna do" was not a question. It was a life lesson, it was years of experience summed up in a succinct phrase, handed down from generation to generation. He knew he had screwed up. He knew it would follow him for the rest of their lives. I think he also knew, like me, that he wasn't going to change, especially at this age; he was wired this way. So... "what're ya gonna do?"

Sometimes you just need to acknowledge shit and move on as best you can.

THE SILVER MAN, AND OTHER TALES OF THE MACABRE

The Adirondacks, and the High Peaks area in particular, are known for their beauty, majesty, difficulty, and blah blah blah. But another thing they have going for them, is some rather unexplainable stuff, that may or may not be filed under "The Paranormal." Some is quite improbably true, more is maybe Urban Legendy, and I'll bet most is just in the heads of the folks that live there, and probably mostly the kids' heads.

Though I know for a fact that adults have active imaginations as well, as evidenced by the conversation I had with the newest owner of the house I grew up in, 30 years after we stopped living there. We were visiting the area on the occasion of my Dad's 80th birthday, so we took a drive out to Mohawk Lake to see the old place, and show our son where I grew up. The owner happened to be home, and invited us to talk for a bit down on the dock at the boathouse.

We chatted for a few minutes about the house and area in general, and then things got a tiny bit weird. The owner asked me about one of the outbuildings on the property, and I said, pointing in the general direction "The one near the barn? Oh, my dad and grandfather built that. Why?"

He gave me a weird look and a "huh." I asked why. He got kind of dodgy at first, as if he couldn't find the words to ask me. Turns out there were all sorts of rumors and theories about the building, one involved the Amish bringing it in on a horse-drawn wagon, and another had a helicopter flying it in and plopping it down.

Really? Stories and rumors… over a glorified shed? A small, one-and-a-half story, hand-framed, 300-square-foot outbuilding? No one was ever even killed in that shed, how did rumors start about how it got there, everybody had sheds, and most folks built stuff by hand in that area. Though I will admit, my dad and grandfather did not muck around. It was a *really* nice shed, hand-made, electricity, sturdy as shit, and clearly built to last. Dad had built it as an office and storage facility for the gear he stocked for his S&R and forest fire needs.

The new owner seemed assuaged by this answer, and we chatted about it no more. I do however, kick myself to this day that I had missed a swell opportunity to breathe some life into a local legend, and for that I will never forgive myself. I am usually tuned in to situations like this, and always loved stirring the pot.

"Yeah, man," I could have said, "No idea... we all woke up one morning, and it was... just...*there*, man!" or maybe even

"*That* shed? Dude, that was the one the Harper kids went into... and never returned from. Go read the 1974 Daily Enterprise article about them," I'd have said, then looked confused and fearful as I turned back to him, "But... but it burned down 25 years ago..."

Legends.

When I was a kid, we had The Johnson House. This was a big gray house about two houses down from where we lived, and at some point, it got into our heads that it was now a vacant, haunted house. "Our heads" means the gang of kids I rode with, random kids who lived up or down our stretch of road. I think it may have included one or more of my brothers and sister too.

There were times when we would all ride our bikes together to see what trouble we could get into, and one of our targets was The Johnson House. Any time you talked with anyone (our ages) there was different story about that house, and at some point you have to – HAVE TO – go check it out for yourself. So we did. In the name of science.

The Johnson House sat at the bottom of a slope, and was backed right up against a granite outcropping, so one could actually – in theory – climb onto the outcropping, and then step right onto the first story roof and climb up to the windows on the second floor – all while being unobserved from the street. Which was okay, until you think that maybe if you disappeared in there, nobody would have known or seen you go in. You could have gone unnoticed for days before someone found your bikes – all rusty and intergrown with weeds – piled at the back corner of the house. And you would become part of the mystery of the house for future generations, which, really, would have been an honor.

So a group of us, armed with nothing more than spunk and misinformation, entered through the back window on the second floor one day. The house *felt* creepy; the dark hallways were *very* spooky, like right out of horror movies spooky, where you could only see so far, and you just *knew* something was going to come out at you from the dark.

We explored anyway, because there were more than one of us, and groups of kids derive their strength from that shit. We crept around cautiously, quietly, eventually making our way to the stairs that led down to the living room area. But that trip down into the bowels of Hell was cut short when one of us very clearly noticed a large coffin in the living room, then quietly announced it to the group. This caused a chain reaction of running away at top speed, and bailing out the back window as fast as we could. We ran or biked to an agreed upon rally spot where we could easily debrief each other, and add that much more to legend of The Johnson House.

Years later, looking back through the fog of time, using the lens of clarity that one forms as an adult that actual knows how things work, I can surmise this much: there was no mystery to The Johnson House other than being an empty house that was maybe or not up for sale. There was no coffin in the living room, it was likely a box or crate left behind when the inhabitants, maybe let's say the Johnsons, left and never came back for it. I will even go so far as to postulate that we as group performed some B&E on a house that quiet people still lived in, or it maybe was even someone's vacation home. Anything else was fear and lies compounding on themselves with some overly creative young minds.

Or... it *was* actually haunted but we were too young to realize how narrowly we escaped with our lives.

Old houses with questionable haunt-status aside, there were plenty of other interesting stories and myths from the North Country: The Lady In The Lake, various Big Footery sightings, Hippie Hijackers, Magical Waters, and even Champ, the prehistoric beast who swims in Lake Champlain. None of them particularly able to be verified or debunked, and certainly nothing that I would have seen first-hand.

Though the Hippie Hijackers might have been spotted at our front door once.

One summer, I recall being in the front yard, which was surrounded on three sides by hedges, so I could not see the road, but I did see our dad come stomping out of the outbuilding shop with an ugly looking mattock in his fist – and he was on a mission – as he lumbered toward the road, bellowing something or other.

Then I heard a vehicle's doors slam, and tires of said vehicle spit gravel as it pulled away from our driveway quickly. Being as shallow a thinker as I was, I didn't really take note of what was happening at the time – Dad had a penchant for stomping, mattock toting, AND bellowing, so it was just a typical Tuesday so far.

Turns out, upon chatting with my oldest brother years later, that *this* was what happened: he was coming back from the lake when a van pulled up. The passenger front seat guy was asking my brother a bunch of questions, apparently keeping him busy, as another guy was leaning out of the back of the van toward him, grinning.

Our dad saw this from the window, grabbed the biggest, most intimidating thing at hand, and stormed out the door. Dad was pretty scary all by himself, let alone stomping toward the road with murder in his eyes, a weapon in his hand and bellowing "CAN I HELP YOU WITH SOMETHING?" Those guys in the van made the right call in bugging out. 'Cause somebody was about to get FUCKED. UP.

Dad phoned a friend with the State Police, and a short time later, they found the van in question abandoned on the side of the road.

So *that* legend may have had some validity.

But one of the most supernaturaliest phenomenonical things that I ever saw was The Silver Man.

When we kids were all still fairly young, I think I was maybe five or six, the house we lived in was being renovated, and for a brief time us three boys shared a room in what was to eventually be my oldest brother's room, 'cause it was bigger. This room was a split-level dealie with a pretty big upper portion, and then a few steps down to a little ante-room with a closet that was situated above the old coal chute. Weird set-up, but old bespoke-built houses tend to be like that, architecture-wise.

Anyhoo, my two brothers slept in beds up in the main room, and I had a bed down in the ante-room that could have collapsed at any minute into the darkness of the abyss. The head of the bed was against the wall, and if I turned on my right side I could see right up into the main room, about the bottom halves of their beds in view. A window was between their beds, and at certain times of the month moonlight filled the room through this window.

One night, I have no idea how late it was, but it was VERY quiet, very still; in fact it was likely that quiet stillness that woke me up. I had turned on my side and looked up into their room, and there at the foot of Frank's bed, in a pool of moonlight, was this Silver Man. He was just sitting – with rather good posture – with his hands on his knees, looking at my brother sleep.

I will say, that this man was not like any man I have ever seen before, and I could not be certain it was one gender or another. It wore no clothes, its body – which looked somewhat like TV static – had no discernible topography that I could see, and the eyes were just black pools. At one point this Silver Man turned and looked right at me, no real emotion or anything even resembling "I'mma eat you next" kind of scariness. Just a "noticing" look; then looked back toward my brother.

Immediately, my special training kicked in, and I did what all kids my age had been instructed to do: I yanked the blankets up over my head, and hoped the Silver Man would be so full from eating my brother(s), it wouldn't mess with me.

I waited the suggested amount of time before bringing the blankets down again, and the Silver Man was gone. My brothers were still there, by-and-large uneaten or even nibbled at. It was a mostly sleepless night for me after that, of course at some point I drifted off, my eyes still opened. The next day I told my brothers about it, and there was a WOW moment or two, and "how cool is that's" going around. As far as I know none of us ever saw anything like that again in the house.

I have no idea what it means, or meant, and nothing seemed to change afterward – like we didn't all the sudden have strange powers or anything, and my brothers are still as dumb as bricks, so there was no mind-meld-enhancement; but it was a really special experience to have as a kid. And it is a nice addition to whatever weird-assery the North Country holds.

The Great Camps that dotted the Adirondacks may have had their ghost stories, and in general there were interesting goings-on all over the place; but for a brief moment in time, Mohawk Lake had the Silver Man. I have no idea if anyone else in the area ever claimed to have been visited by him, or seen him. But he definitely visited my brother. I saw it with my own eyes.

THE DEATH OF RUBY LACROIX

Death. It's coming for you. Whether you are young or old, the concept of death pretty much touches everyone at some point, and affects them in different ways. If you grew up on a farm, or in the rugged type of area we grew up in, you may have dealt with some kind of death every day. Whether animals getting sick, or becoming a food source for an outside predator, or becoming a food source for you – there was a lot of death out there.

Don't even get me started on the human deaths in rural areas, between drinking and driving, drinking and fighting, drinking and hunting, or drinking and snowmobiling. This is to say nothing of the non-drinking fatalities of falling into a piece of farm equipment, or being run over by a piece of farm equipment, fighting with a drunken piece of farm equipment – well let's just say there were plenty of opportunities to either be dead, hear about death, or be death-adjacent, and I am sure everyone had their druthers about which they would prefer.

I'd hear about deaths all the time, either in the news, portions of conversations, from other kids' gossip, etc. Most of the time it didn't really register with me. It was just a thing that happened, to people who I never even heard of.

Then there were the close encounters of the first kind, where someone you actually knew died – a neighbor, close friend, close friend's family member, or one of your own. It is one thing to hear stories about your great grandfather passing away after wrasslin' a mountain lion, and quite another to watch your own grandmother fall ill and pass away. Once it happened to someone you knew, it wasn't long, no matter how old you were, before you started thinking about mortality.

My dad always had some sort of search and rescue thing going on, dragging some dumbass hikers off a mountain, out of a lake, or maybe finding a plane wreck in a remote area. Sometimes he would aid the State Troopers in a manhunt, which also required the retrieval of a body or bodies. I'd hear about this first via my dad – not directly to me of course – but I could hear him on the phone, or with the rangers that would gear up in our driveway. And then I would hear the local news version of the same stories when it hit the tv or radio. It was a bit weird having "insider" info about these things before they were announced on the news, and it certainly wasn't anything I ever bragged about.

There was this one particular story that hit sort of close to home for me. There was a mental health facility over near Tupper Lake I think, and one night a patient escaped and abducted someone. The abductee's body was found later, and then the manhunt ensued, and they caught the perp. Then I found out – via newspaper headlines or radio – that the perp was a former Boy Scout.

I was a current Boy Scout, or Cub Scout more specifically. My mind immediately went into a version of what happened, but the criminal was now wearing a full scout uniform with green and red knee socks and knew how to tie knots, and tell which way north was by looking closely at where the moss was growing on the tree.

As I got older and thought back on that whole situation, I realized of course that this was just some guy who had major psychological issues and, unfortunately, he was able to figure out an escape from that facility, and led police and rangers on a manhunt after committing a heinous crime.

So why, when the news described this person, why did they glom onto the fact that he was a "former Boy Scout?" It literally had nothing to do with the proceedings at hand – it just created an image in people's minds that didn't do anything to help the situation. All it did was put "psychiatric patient," "murderer," and "Boy Scout" all in the same line. Whatever the circumstances, somebody that was the same thing I was at the time, had caused someone else to be dead.

Farm accidents, meal prep, unfortunate hikers, and murders aside, the first incident that for whatever reason really drove home for me the idea of the finality of death, was Ruby LaCroix. Ruby was a friend of my mother, I think she was a patient first. Anyway, she was ill, breast cancer I learned later, and she got on my radar when my mother told us we had to go make a visit to her and her family because she was very sick, and Mom couldn't leave me at home alone while she visited.

The visit – for me – was pretty unnoteworthy. I think I played with kids close to my age during the visit, while Mom helped with Ruby. There I was in the house, with this person right over there, and playing with the kids – and then poof, the next day my mom says we have a funeral to attend, and it is for Ruby.

So the next thing I know, I'm wearing tiny "fancy" clothes with a bow tie, and sitting in a church on NOT Sunday, but it kind of feels like Sunday cause I'm in church. Then the doors at the back of the house opened, with their muted thuds, and the sound of something heavy being wheeled in hit my ears. It wasn't long before a large box was rolled past me on the way to the front of church, and I asked my mom what was up.

"That's Ruby LaCroix," she said, and nothing else.

Welllllll... what the hell do I do with that? Inside that box was that person I just saw a few days ago? That's weird. She seemed fine the other day. Why are these people crying? Why is all the talking up front from the guy in the robe so solemn and heavy? Oh look, there's those kids I played with. Lot of thoughts going on, but not a whole lot of understanding from me.

Then the box got wheeled to a really long car, and I thought, well nifty that they have cars that can accommodate a box that size, but why not just use a truck? The box got taken to a cemetery, and we followed close behind, driving really slow. The box got carried to the side of a big hole in the ground, and then lowered in, and then covered up, and then we went home eventually.

I know my mother sat me down and explained what happened at one point, because she did that a lot – I just for the life of me don't recall the words because I was too young I suppose. But it made sense to me. It usually did, my mom was good with explaining things to us kids.

So when I heard a few years later on that my mother's father had passed away, I knew what it meant. I was able to place a face and a voice and a feeling to the word Death, and feel whatever it was I felt now that it was someone I actually knew rather well. But these were adults, and well, as a kid, you just figure that adults die, especially old ones or sick ones. Certainly not your own parents though.

But then one Tuesday morning my mom came into my room and told me that one of my best friends – Jake Kawen from down the street – had just passed away. Jake was a few years ahead of me in school, in fact I think he had all but graduated from high school when I was eight. But we got along really well, he was a very quiet and even-keeled kid, he could play the electric bass, and most of all he put up with me. My sister was friends with Jake's sister, and they lived one house away from the Catholic church.

I would ride my bike over and hang out, greeted by a smile and a "Hey man, what you up to today?" Jake would play cool riffs on his bass, like the theme from

Barney Miller or Smoke On The Water, and so forth; or I'd help him rake leaves, or some other chore. Was weird thinking that he was no longer around.

It was especially bad when I found out he died from an accident, a completely avoidable situation, where he drowned. I knew Jake couldn't swim, he was great at every sport, but water just terrified him. Even with that fear, he would still go down to the beach with me to keep an eye on me if no one else was available.

"Yeah man, let's go wading," he would say; he'd never say "let's go swimming."

So when the dock at the back of the restaurant Jake worked at collapsed, and all the other staff fell into the lake, and were able to pull themselves, laughing, out of the water; Jake was the only one that didn't make it out. He had panicked pretty hard in some really shallow water – had he just stood up, he would have lived.

THAT put me off swimming for years, which irked the shit out of my dad, because being a Navy man, having a son that didn't swim was a harsh thing to deal with. I didn't really get back into swimming until our kids were learning to swim; because like HELL I was going to let them into a pool or lake if I couldn't be in there with them. Death may come for us all at one time or another, but I wanted to make sure our kids wouldn't be visited directly simply because no one was there to realize that they were too afraid to simply stand up in shallow water.

I have had more than enough death incidents in the ensuing years, and it has become more and more famil-iar to me, but it also does not bother me so much when

I think about it showing up in my own personal space at some point.

I would prefer I *not* see it coming. It would be real great if I could just get hit by a bus out of nowhere or something – I really did not enjoy watching my paternal grandmother waste away, completely sound mind, knowing what was coming. GAAAAHHHH, no thank you.

Personally, I really do understand that everybody shuffles off at some point or another; I just have issues with the execution of the transaction – for lack of a better term. Sudden illness, that could work. A sudden, quick drop off into the ether would be fine. A hero's send-off? That'd be something, charging into a burning something or other to save another person. The thing is, I'm more of the chickenshit type, so that option is likely off the table. A ridiculous death might be okay. You know, a safe falling on my head, like that poor guy on Bagel Street from the Susquehanna Hats story. That sort of thing. For me anyway – that would be just fine.

And I would hope that those I leave behind would be able to appreciate the ridiculosity of the event. But no matter what it is, when it shows up for me, I hope I just find it interesting and not too terrifying or sad. Not like I have a choice, but I do have my druthers.

tHE HOUSE tHAt FrED BUiLt

When you get older, you acquire more realistic ideas about owning your own house. Things like mortgages, property taxes, repair costs, upkeep, replacing major appliances and what not take up most of your day. That beautiful, quaint or interesting home you thought you'd have one day becomes more of a nightmare and less of a dream for some folks. But often, thoughts will drift back to another time and place, when one didn't have to worry about the actual day-to-day of owning a home.

I imagine most people have dreams of places they have lived before, and I am no different. One of the most frequent pre-current-home places I dream about is that old house in Mohawk Lake. I know at least one of my siblings does as well, my oldest brother. He visits whenever he is in the neighborhood. Me, I've only really been back a handful of times. But when I have dreams about hanging out in one of my favorite places on the planet, it is usually that house, and the surrounding area.

Unlike some of the communities in that region, Mohawk Lake the hamlet actually sits right on Mohawk Lake the lake. Nearby Saranac Lake the village does not sit on Saranac Lake the lake, even though Saranac Lake the lake is quite close by. Farther out, Lake Placid the village does not sit on Lake Placid the lake; and furthermore, Lake Placid the lake in NY is not the lake Lake Placid of the movie Lake Placid where the crocodile eats people. And none of these Lake Placids are the Lake Placid In Queensland, Australia – where they actually *do* have crocodiles.

This area is nuanced. Crocodileless.

Our old house was built around the time of the American Civil War, by German immigrants Munchen by name. Froederick Munchen built the house with his son and family using the materials available on that sloping land that led down to that wonderful little 940 acre lake in Franklin County. The Munchen family lived there until 1966 when this little family from Cranberry Lake, NY moved in because the father of that family was the newly-appointed ranger for the area.

The great-granddaughter of Fred Munchen, Margo, still owned the house, and she lived there for a bit while my family also occupied the house. She then moved into a trailer right across the road so she could still be close to this house that clearly meant a lot to her as well. I still have a few photographs of that old house from shortly after it was built, even one with Margo's grandfather standing at a vegetable stand on the front lawn.

The huge barn at the back of our main house area was just as old and haunted-looking as the house. Haunteder, because it was left mostly unpainted, and so the weathered wood siding was all shades of gray, and the two windows that looked down at the house were black-paned without interior lights on.

The first floor was jammed with work benches and what I can only call "a great deal of crap." I will note here that "crap" was a term of endearment for all the stuff we had that was useful, but may not have looked like it at first blush. We eventually remodeled that floor to have two tricked-out horse stalls, only one that ever housed a pony. The pony was an asshole, it bucked me into a wood pile one time and chewed some of the 4x4s in its stall down to 2x2s. We got rid of it. We don't talk about it.

Those stalls then went on to good use as pens for the chickens, turkeys and duck hatchlings we got in early spring. A heated tent-shaped aluminum brooder on the floor would keep them warm as they grew in the coldish early months until they could be relocated to their permanent homes. Ah the aroma of heated bird poop in the morning, let me tell you.

The second floor was filled to the gills with lumber, both new and old, and also some scrap metal and assorted other things that could be re-used, re-purposed, or cannibalized as needed. A big square vertical hatch opened out just over the main barn door, and on occasion we mused at jumping just to see if we'd break anything useful, such as a leg or something. I honestly cannot say if I ever tried the jump, but I have un-verifiable visions of one of my brother's jumping once. Not sure it was very pleasant.

This big old house had a lot of history and a fair amount of charm and mystery. While renovating it, we were exposed to the way houses were built a hundred years ago: rough cut lumber, likely hand-sawn, square nails, newspapers for insulation, slat and plaster drywall technique with pig hair as a binder. An attic held together by bats and ghosts, and a cellar that was the last rest-stop – kind of like a Luv's – on the way up from Hell.

That damn cellar. A lot of our firewood was stored down there in the winter, and our canned vegetables and fruits lined the shelves against the wall and staircase. But the light switch was at the very bottom of the stairs. Just as you stepped off the last step, you had to reach your hand out into the dark to find the string that hung from the naked bulb socket.

Going down into the dark of the cellar, you knew at some point there would be light; so in comparison to going up, that was alright. Going up? You had to yank off the light, and make it upstairs before the Devil got you.

It was such a harrowing way to live as a child, never knowing when that clammy, scaly hand would find your hand in the dark before you could turn the light on and dispel all the evil. And then having to outrun it once the light was off again. Why couldn't Dad just have installed a damn light switch at the top of the stairs? Did he do that shit on purpose? I mean, he renovated the entire rest of the damn house – what was wrong with him?

The attic was not quite as bad, though scary enough in its own right. I am nearly 100% certain that the ghosts of a lot of people lived in that attic – and they probably all spoke German, which was even scarier. I could literally feel them any time I looked through the items that were left up there. The boxes of old photos, the clothes, the *things*. Old Kodak bellows cameras, WWI weapons and gear, that freakishly haunted wardrobe at the east end of the attic that whispered our names. YEEEEESH, I get oogy just thinking about it.

And the bats. Actual, live bats lived up there, and at least once, I think maybe twice, a bat had made its way down the attic stairs and was waiting when I opened the door – which was two steps outside my room's door. The attic door made a right angle with my brother Chris' door, but it opened toward mine.

When both doors were opened (the attic's and mine), the bat would flitty flit flit across that two-step expanse, into my room. Confused by the light, it would just zig zag all over my room until we could chase it out with a broom, either back into the attic, or out an open window.

The house was not particularly modern when our family moved in. The kitchen stove was wood-burning, and there was a large metal kerosene heater that took up much of the cave that was the living room. It felt like there were so many nooks and crannies in that house, each filled with mystery and weirdness; and you could practically feel the weight of the history in it. I loved it.

The roof was multi-leveled, not just one roof that covered the whole thing, and it was made of corrugated tin. It was maybe twenty or twenty five feet at the highest point? The roof itself was a fun-filled deathtrap of a playground as well. We ran around on that roof all the time, climbing up a low-slope here, sliding down a steep pitch there.

There were summers when ill-advised children, mostly boys, would stuff their school bags with filled water balloons, and run and hop around on those multi-roof-layers throwing balloons at each other.

What great fun, to not be plagued by the facts that wet corrugated tin was no match for the well-worn soles of last season's Converse All-Star high tops. That any false, water-lubricated step would likely be our last, and we would squeakily slide to the edge, then plummet to the ground with a wet splarch, maybe lucky enough to crack our spines on that one granite boulder that sat just off the back porch, where all the wild mint grew. WHEEEEE!

In the summers I could open one of my front-facing windows and climb out on to the roof and stare up at the sky and stars, or look down at the lake on bright-mooned nights. Sometimes my brother and I would borrow Dad's navy binoculars, which were like see-a-pimple-on-an-ant-five-miles-away-strong, and we'd sit on the roof and he would show me where the Andromeda galaxy was and other spaceful shit like that.

In the winter, the heavy snow would slide off that roof to form huge mounds right in front of the house, where we would later tunnel into it to make snow forts, maybe being smart enough to fortify the diggings with water that we would spray-on to freeze the walls. Not being engi-neers, or possessing a great deal of foresight as to pos-sible outcomes, the danger of the eventual cave-ins that might bury us alive posed no real threat.

If we were lucky, sometimes at night, we'd hear some weird noise from outside on the roof. If you knew what you were listening to, you'd know that very soon you'd hear a muffled whoosh and subsequent FLOOMPH! As the foot-or-more-deep snow from the roof slid off en masse and landed on the already four-foot deep pile below. YES! There shall be a cave digging on the morrow!

I did have one cave collapse on me once. I was solo digging in a heap, which was created by the snow-blowing activities of Dad or older brother next to the workshop/office out-building next to the house. My dog – I want to say our Dalmatian – was helping. I had dug in one side, made a good-sized main cavern, and was just digging out the other side when it just collapsed on me. No idea why, I followed the carefully-calculated-and-measured plans to the letter. I should have sued the architect.

Anyway, the snow covered me up to my shoulders, with just one arm and head outside. My dog immediately ran over and started to dig me out. I could almost hear it growling under it's breath "I *told* you this would happen, you have no idea of what you are doing, nobody listens to the dog..."

The pup helped get me to where I could finally use both my arms and finish digging myself out. Well, I'm never going to do *that* again, I vowed, as I started to dig my next cave around the other side of the house.

There was a trail through the trees that led from the second clearing – where the pigs and big garden were – up to what we cleverly named "The Third Clearing." This was a few acres of meadow-like land that I vaguely remember us clearing when we moved in. I have a fuzzy memory of sitting in the back of the little blue wagon that hooked up to our Ford tractor – this was a little riding lawnmower-type tractor, not a big heavy industrial sort. I would just enjoy the ride and watch as the grownups cleared the brush and smaller trees. That meadow was later overrun with wild blueberry bushes, and we could spend days on end picking them and still not make a dent.

For more winter fun, on moonlit nights (and some-times moonless ones), we'd play snowmobile tag on the trails that led from that meadow farther down into the backwoods. We'd speed through trails that were barely wide enough for our Evinrude and Ski-Doo, then pull just off the trail, turn off our lights, and hide amongst the trees until the other sled whizzed by and stopped, and the passenger would point and shout "GOT YOU!"

Even with the bright moonlight, it was DARK back there, everything that wasn't white as snow (which looked light grey) just looked like shadows. The snow-mobile lights playing through the trees creating highly-contrasted images, animated by the jarring bumps and jags of the trail, added to the surreal play. The memorable smell of the oil-and-gas two-stroke engine emissions still find their way into my brain every now and again.

I can not even *imagine* what mayhem could have been wrought by hitting a thirty-foot pine tree doing 25 mph on an open-air gas-powered sled with no seat belts.

SOOOOO many OSHA violations.

The land around the house and property was dotted with fruit trees, some that were planted on purpose, some that clearly just grew out of some seed that got tossed. There were so many trees to climb; I could spend hours reading a book on the wide, horizontal branches of a favorite tree on the trail leading back into the woods. A few enormous granite boulders covered with soft moss dotted the land; between those and the two pump houses on the hill, there was plenty of space to stretch out on, stare up at the leaves and clouds, and daydream.

Is it any wonder I miss that old house? Is it any wonder I have thought more than once about buying it again one day? I do, and I have... until I think about the upkeep, repairs and replacements on a 160-year-old house. For now, I'll just keep visiting it in my dreams, thank you.

DAMN FINE GRANDPARENTING

We saw a set of grandparents all the time. That is not to say that we had visions, or were "seeing things" that looked like grandparents, though that would have been really interesting; but rather we had one set of grandparents we saw a lot, and another set that we rarely saw. In fact, that one set came to live with us shortly before my parents got divorced, and may have even hastened their divorcenning.

My dad's parents, hardy stock from Russian and Hungarian descent, were the grandparents of choice. Not necessarily *our* choice as the grandchildren, though we really loved seeing them, but they were the ones we saw the most. Whether driving down to NYC/Yonkers to see them or having them drive up to see us. They were the grandparents that would show up with a new color TV, or boxes of homemade or Yonkers Deli foods, and one time even a carload of new bikes for all us kids. They brought us a dog once too – a black lab named Mac. *That* was a dog, very smart, a lot of fun. These were the grandparents we saw the most, and what was generally acknowledged when any one of us said "Grandpa" or "Grandma."

What was the reason for this one-sided grandparent situation? I am not quite sure, and could not say with any certainty, but since I love a good story, I will share this:

One day my mother's parents were on their way up to see us. The trip up from Yonkers, back in that day, was a five or six hour car ride; because cars were big, heavy juggernauts that used 26 gallons of gas per mile. And also stopping to ask directions or using a map was not going to happen.

Our dad was outside working on the house, and I vaguely recall being outside when this happened, though since memory is not a reliable witness, I will recuse myself as having seen it for sure – though even if I did, I would not have understood what I was seeing. But I did understand my father, so it would have tracked if all I did was *hear* about it, even at six years old.

The car containing my mother's parents arrived after that long hot trip. My maternal grandfather was a kindly (sarcasm) old man about five foot six who could turn forest animals to stone just by clearing that gravel-and-broken-glass throat of his, and indeed this was likely something he would have done for sport had the idea of enjoyment been anywhere in his playbook. He got out of the car and walked up to meet our father, and they faced each other. A welcoming greeting between a father and a son-in-law, what could possibly go wrong?

I can imagine there was only time to say a few short, angry words on either side, but heads were jerking in and out at each other like half-speed, belligerent pigeons. Hands were flying, fingers were pointed – it was *not* a pleasant "hello, how are you, John, great to see you Frank" sort of moment. Then my Maternal Grandfather immediately turned around, went back to the car, got in, and they drove back home – all of this before my mother even got outside to welcome them.

And we never had a visit from them again. We went to visit, but they never came back up. *That* really sort of explains a lot about my family dynamic in a nut shell.

Those grandparents had their good points, as I'm sure most people do. They were Austrian-Polish-Russian types. Maternal Grandpa, who was built like a cinder block, was a repair man for anything electric. ANY-THING. If it plugged into the wall, ran on batteries, or drew power from some Tesla-assed lightning-shrouded silver ball, he could fix it. His back porch was packed to the gills with TVs, radios, toasters, tons of appliances and stuff. He also collected coins and paper money from different countries, and had an absolute *love affair* with drinking, smoking cigars, and shouting at children.

He had a dog named Charlie, a mutt who he was surprisingly fond of and patient with, and he taught that dog to talk. Grandpa would be coming downstairs in the morning, Charlie would be sitting at the base of the stairs, waiting for him. Grandpa would stop at the top of the first turn landing, look down at Charlie and say – in as singsongy a voice as you get out of a steel shredder rendering an old chevy engine – "Good morning, Charlie. I said…. Good morning Charlie."

And that dog – and this time I *did* see it with my own ears – that dog said "Good Morning." Now, it wasn't proper English and diction like some actor from the UK affecting an American accent. It was actually closer to Scooby-Doo or Astro, but by God, that dog said "ooood marnnee." Also in his vocabulary were "Ri rove rou" and some other phrase. And that was Grandpa on mom's side: could get his dog to talk, would just as soon make schnitzel of the grandchildren.

Maternal Grandma was a quietish woman, not much of a talker with us, but friendly and pleasant and always had a smile at the ready. Her personal catch phrase "I'm fine," was literally the last words out of her mouth when she passed.

This was a heavy Yonkers-accented "I'm Fine," we're talking about. Not a simple brush-off retort, but a two-word phrase akin to Texas' "Bless your heart," that could be wielded like a thesaurus entry if you knew what you were listening to. A drawn out "Aym Fiiiiiiiiiiinnnnee," spoke volumes about how she viewed her past and likely felt about her current situation.

Our favorite thing to look forward to when visiting Grandma, was the fact the she would sit us in front of the (at least) four TVs that always seemed to occupy the corner of the room over there between the front windows and the fireplace. She'd let us watch as many shows at the same time as we wanted, and lovingly fed us the finest quality Pringles and Hi-C she could afford. And I'm not talking about the lame-grandma handful-of-pringles-on-a-napkin kind of treat. This was whole-sleeve-per-kid level. She should have won a medal. For that, and for living with grandpa for as many years as she did without running a hat pin through him.

My paternal grandmother was something – *man* she could cook and bake. Holidays would not have been the same without the nut rolls and cookies, and egg cheese, and donuts and whatever she made that she brought huge boxes of. Her regular every day foods were simple and fantastic. Goulash, corn beef and cabbage, sauerkraut and kielbasa – bozhe moye. She tried to dispatch us with food, and we gladly bought a plot and headstone and wrote our own obituaries.

Now, grandma did have a tad of a temper, so we know where that came from, and where Dad got it. Grandma could be quick to anger, and tardy on the recoup – but she did have a great smile, and a pretty decent laugh. Just don't use too much toilet paper in one bathroom visit, or you might get the back of her hand, or more likely the back of Dad's hand if she ratted on us. Which she did.

The only Russian I ever learned was from when grandma and grandpa would sit at the kitchen table and play gin rummy at night. I'd sneak out of my room and stick my head through the banister to hear what I could. It was usually grandma talkin' smack about us kids, and how difficult it was to do the work that needed doing in the house – in Russian – so it sounded even worse. Some words were familiar, so it was easy to figure out the context. Grandpa, a rather smart man, would nod and "uh-huh" and "mmm-hmm" a lot.

Paternal grandpa was the nicest guy on earth. Extremely friendly, very sharp, no bullshit. He just quietly took care of bi'ness. I learned a lot from him in a positive way – how to do some woodwork, how to fix cars, how to make, edit and appreciate film. Every holiday, or any other night when the mood took him, grandpa would set up the portable movie screen, get out the Bell + Howell projector and the old 8mm movies and we'd have a little show.

Some of the films were from the 40s or earlier, so the celluloid broke a lot. He would patiently show me how to trim off the bad ends and tape the strips back together, even show me how he did stop-motion animated credits for some of the movies.

But my favorite movie-related story about Grandpa, was one night, while we were visiting them in their third-story walk-up on Williams Street in Yonkers, this movie came on, and it had no sound, and no color. The color wasn't really an issue because we had always had a black and white TV, but the lack of sound was interesting.

Anyway, I couldn't have been more than five years old at the most, but he sat me on his knee and we watched that old silent movie start to finish, and I was just *riveted* to it. The emotion, the tone, the feeling, the images – I was just hooked on it. I have no memory of anything he may have said to me about what was going on – I just remember sitting there watching with him as he introduced me to German Expressionist Cinema via The Cabinet of Dr. Caligari. Might have seemed like an odd choice for grandparent to pick for watching with a very young grandchild, but it suited me just fine.

One of my biggest regrets in life was that I did not spend more time with either set of grandparents, and talk to them more about those sides of the family. But knowing what I know, neither side would have been very forthcoming with any info about the family tree. My paternal grandfather frequently let little drops of family stories leak out when we talked while working, and some of these stories were instrumental in me finding the correct family members when I looked them up years later online. The other three just weren't very talkative about it, and my mother's family seemed like they *really* didn't want anyone to find their people at all.

The growling and drinking, the lack of conversation, the angry outbursts and the poorly-chosen movies aside, I miss both sets. But I am reminded of them constantly when I look at the photos on the wall, see a physical resemblance in my reflection, or do something that I know I learned from one of them. All things said and done, it was all just some damn-fine grandparenting.

HELLO, MY NAME IS MARK

One bully can ruin your whole day. A truckload of bullies can ruin your whole life; or at least make a lot of days an absolute chore. One thing most people do not think about is that, like everyone else you meet in the world, bullies can help shape your life as well.

Mohawk Lake and the surrounding area had its share of bullies, some of them age appropriate, some fairly indiscriminate, nearly all of them shared the same M.O. It is easy to spot a bully after you have had extensive field research.

Eventually, of course, you figure out that some bullies are just the result of shit flowing downhill to a weaker person. Sometimes they are just mean-spirited people who like to make someone else's life miserable. Sometimes they feel like they have no control over their lives, so they decide to foist control on someone that *will* do what they want, such as an easy Mark.

A Mark can be spotted a mile away by a Bully – it's in the way the Mark carries themselves. They tend to look down a lot, avoiding eye-contact, their body language says "I am trying to be tiny, so as not to be noticed," they tend to shrink from conflict of any kind, they *never* fight back.

Here's a freebie for you as concerns bullies: Fight back. You may get your nose pinned to your ear, but you will show you are nobody's punching bag. Fight back. Once bullying *you* becomes too much like a job, they will look for someone else. Bullying, by and large, is a crime of opportunity.

One winter on the playground, I got surrounded once again by the impromptu gladiatorial containment ring that was formed by a schoolyard full of kids eager to watch the latest train wreck that was Dorchak vs Bully. And not just any bully; this bully was the youngest cousin to a family of bullies who I guess needed his Blood-In to join the gang properly. I seemed like an easy Mark, I mean I was already a known quantity, right?

He taunted, he laughed, he actually motioned for cheers from the crowd as he prepared to pound me. Not one f-ing teacher in sight. Then he got this LOOK on his face. This smug, asshole look that I had seen so many times before on my arch-nemesis, his cousin, and many other schoolyard thugs. Frankly, I had had just about enough of that shit. This kid didn't even earn it, he was just riding his cousin's coattails. So you know what?

WHOP.

Right in the jaw.

My fist was back in its holster before I even realized what I did. The *eyes* on that guy as he looked at me like he had offered me a puppy and for some reason I stabbed him in the face with a trident in response. He held his jaw for a minute or two as the crowd, their jaws also open, started to disperse.

"Yeah, man," I thought to myself, "you want another one, cause I can give yo…" my interior victory speech was cut short by a voice behind me.

"Mr. Dorchak, Principal's Office, NOW."

Didn't really matter to me much. I was on my way to understanding how bullies operated. It is a nuanced thing, and sometimes almost awe-inspiring to watch.

"Hey Dorchak, nice book bag," you'd hear on your way to class. Then a hand would grab said bag, and YEET, down the stairs it would go. Simple, reliable, never-fail gag. The ol' Snatch-and-Chuck, with the Misdirectional Compliment at the lead. A finely-crafted play for the ages. And it's quick; any responsible adult in the nearby vicinity would likely never have seen it happen. All they'd see was some schmuck kid with low motorskills picking up his books at the foot of the stairs, because he had clearly dropped them himself. Classic.

"Hey Dorchak, I heard you said something about me in math class." This wasn't a question, not even a rhetorical one; it was a statement. This was the Bait-n-Bash maneuver, wherein a scenario was presented that supposedly *you* created, and now you would pay dearly for. Not very disarming, like with the Snatch-and-Chuck, but effective in its ability to immediately instill fear and self-doubt in the bushwhacked Mark.

"Tell me what you said," they'd smirk again.

"I… I…didn't say anyth…"

"TELL ME WHAT YOU SAID."

This Bait-n-Bash is usually followed immediately by a Grab-and-Shove, typically against a wall where the Mark could then be surrounded by a semi-circle of toadies, yes-men, and apprentice bullies eager to learn at the hands of a Master Bullist.

With the Bait-n-Bash, the bully would get added enjoyment out of the Mark, who is taken off-guard, stumbling about for an answer as they tried ridiculously to figure out what it was they said, thinking that perhaps they had accidentally blurted something. We know through years of study that this simply wasn't true, it was just a clever ruse to confuse and hobble before the strike – which the Bully could now punctuate with a mocking stutter.

"Uhh… uhh… uhh… You think you're funny?" they'd say, followed by a solid Gut-Punch.

The Gut-Punch was always a good move, as it left no real evidence that it was ever there to begin with. A sore stomach could easily be faked by a Mark that chose to tattle; a split lip showed that indeed, *something* had come in contact with a face, perhaps triggering an investigation.

The great thing about these encounters, was that they could last as long as the Bully wanted. The One-and-Done Gut-Punch could easily be the end if the Bully noticed a playground monitor walking their way, whereupon they simply sauntered off, walking on the clouds that were the back-slaps and cheers from their entourage.

For a more robust experience, for those needing more than a simple contact high, the whole scenario could be extended with some well-placed "Huh? Huh? What did you say's?" or "try saying it again to my face's" or the real paralyzer "Apologize to me and I'll let you go's." That last one always got great guffaws from the Gang, as it was the most difficult for the Mark to deal with: apologizing for something you didn't even do. Saying "I'm sorry," to the one who's gonna pound you anyway? Magnificent. Genius.

But the one absolute pinnacle of a Bully's abilities was the way in which they knew how to *not* get caught. Even with the red flag that was a group of toadies constantly attending their shows, they never seemed to get caught in the act. When confronted at any point by a teacher or adult, all the Bully had to do was look innocent – if it was a sort of situation where both parties were questioned at the same time – and say something like "I don't know what *he* saw, but it wasn't me."

Now I know that this inability to point the finger – on the part of the Mark – was based on two things that no self-respecting Mark could do anything about: A) abject fear of retaliation, or B) the knowledge they may have been a *Mark*, but they certainly were not a *Narc*.

By the way, the kids weren't the only bullies at school, got to give some adults their props as well. There were quite a few teachers who gave some students – by some I mean me – a run for the money as well. The way they just always assumed it was Me any time something happened in a five-mile radius.

A funny picture of the teacher on the chalkboard?

"Mr. Dorchak, Principal's office."

The annoying teacher's glasses went missing, causing her to call her husband to bring her spare pair from home?

"Mr. Dorchak, you just earned a trip to the Principal's office."

Somebody wadded up paper and jammed it up in the teacher's little desk bell, because she rang the damn thing like her paycheck was based on pay-per-ding?

"Mr. Dorchak…"

Now in all fairness, I was TOTALLY guilty of all those things. I was constantly doing shit like that. I just didn't like the way I was the go-to for absolutely everything that happened right out of the chute. I mean, I was good, but I statistically could not have been responsible for *everything*. That's profiling.

But that's also known as making one's bed and then lying in it. Set-it-and-forget-it, that's the small town way. You do anything in a small town that garners any notice, and *that* is your label for the rest of your life. *Especially* when most people just don't want to be hampered by thinking and reasoning, or perhaps figuring out that not everything is as it appears.

Even as a kid, I got that pretty quick.

So when, in ninth grade, I was tagged for something I did in Mr. Sloppymushmouth's boring-ass Algebra class one day, I accepted my punishment gracefully, and showed up for lunchtime detention. I sat there and did my homework after listening to Mr. Lazysloppyspeechpattern's lecture, and when the time was up half-way through lunch, I left class without a word to him.

And that's when a couple of the most ridiculously coincidental, one might even say circumstantial, things happened.

As I was walking out of the class, a guy I knew was walking out of the class across the hall, we nodded at each other, "Hey," I said, as I turned the opposite way to head toward the exit doors at the end of the hall. I saw some other kid grabbing books from his locker, then slammed the door shut rather hard, walked two steps, and dropped all his books on the floor.

None of this sounds like a particularly big deal. But three seconds later I heard Mr. I'mjusttoolazytoformcoherentword's voice from behind me.

"Mizder Dorshak, how abou you come ba here and schit ou the res of your lunsh hour." A statement, not a question.

I was genuinely flabbergasted, what could I possibly have even had time to do to piss him off in the last ten seconds? I literally turned round and asked "What? What did I do now?" His stupid beet-red, Doug Henning moustachioed-faced didn't even move when he talked, *that's* how little he cared to shift his mouth when he spoke. His words always sounded like someone trying to wipe up spilled chili from a tile counter top with a paper bag.

"I jush her you yell at shomeone and then her you schlam them agains the wall, and knog thrr boogs don" he slopped. "Now get ba in her befo I give you three mor daysh of detentn."

I saw red, but I also knew not to piss-off the Adults, because they could make things even harder on you than the Kids could. I sauntered, with great attitudinal strides, back to my seat, plopped down, and just sat there staring at the top of that jackass's head as he graded papers for the next 30 minutes. This event was the initial one that led me to notice this behavior in the future, the unjust persecution of innocent people simply because it was the easy path. The Passive Bully, the Bully of Convenience.

Sure, I could have said something to someone, but as they say, Life is so unfair. I had made a reputation at school, and I simply had to live with it. Besides, even if I had tried to get my dad to do something about it, maybe go talk to the teacher or administration, it wouldn't have mattered. He never had my back, ever.

"You deserved it, didn't you." He'd say. A statement, not a question.

"No, what happened was…" I'd start.

"You deserved it, didn't you."

"Dad, it wasn't me…"

"YOU DESERVED IT, DIDN'T YOU." He said louder, and more definitively. As if trying to blot out my words and shove his words down my throat.

"Yeah, Dad," I'd say finally, defeated, "Yeah I did."

Pleased with himself, he'd turn and walk away, happy that I finally realized he was right, and knew my place.

The only thing missing in that scenario was the ol' Grab-and-Shove.

But the Gut-Punch was enough.

tHAT'S (SMALL TOWN) ENTERTAINMENT

One might think, living in a tiny little spot on the map, that there was very little to do in the way of entertainment. Well, there are two schools of thought on that subject: yes and no. We definitely did not grow up in a Hallmark movie town, but there was stuff to do just the same.

While it is true that there were only maybe two local TV stations and then double that with Canadian stations, if you had a fancy TV, like our neighbor did, the kind with the UHF circular antenna that attached via its own console, you could reach maybe a half dozen other channels as well.

When my brother would house-sit for our neighbor, I would go over at night and we could reach a New York

City station – Channel 5, WNEW – to be specific. Home of the Creature Features, where they would run all the old Hammer Films of Dracula, The Mummy, Frankenstein and the like; along with whatever other cheesy Dr.-Phibes-ian Godzilla-esque The-House-That-Dripped-Bloodsy type movies.

These movies came on typically late at night – well late for me anyway – Friday and or Saturday. We'd sit and watch them, just enthralled at the gore and depravity that took place from these monsters, and houses, and demented men of science that either should have known better, or were justified, if not a weency bit indiscriminate in their quest for revenge. Dr. Phibes was particularly creepy and sinister, because he could look like a regular person, then BAM – he'd bake your dogs and make you eat them.

When these movies were over, my brother would say "WOW – that was scary, can you imagine if that was real? Holy cow, they could just grab folks in the dark and murder everyone in this town. Welp, good night!" At which point he would throw open the door and unceremoniously kick my ass out into the damp, dark, street-lightless night and slam the door behind me.

Then, like some seasoned ship captain, I'd have to navigate using the stars and light-house beacon method, where I'd have to walk across the road, just focusing on the one or two lit windows that might be in our house maybe 300 feet away.

Did he NOT understand how dangerous that was? Of course he did. What a dick. Full disclosure, we did eventually get a street light installed, and it was right near our neighbor's place, so there was a pool of light there. But my brother had no way of knowing that was coming some years down the road, so I stand by my assessment.

When we were left at the mercy of our own house for TV entertainment, it was not so groovy. The two local stations we got had boring programming that cut off promptly at midnight and then we were left with a weird test pattern containing lines and circles and configurations of varying widths of stripes, all topped by a gray scale image of a native American wearing a many-feathered headdress. Okay, maybe we got more than two stations, though that may have been after we got our first color TV set in the mid 70s, which was better able to pick up the waves.

Those waves were sucked out of thin air by the standard-issue aluminum fish-bone antenna that stood at the top of a metal pole just outside the window of our living room. The pole was set into the ground at the corner of the house, but when the wind got hold of the business end, it would often move enough so that it eventually spun pretty easy.

This allowed us to, when necessary, climb out onto the roof through my room's window, grab the pole with both hands, and manually adjust it for a better viewing experience. And yes, this happened even when it was raining and lightninging out, in fact *especially* when it was storming, as storms tended to move the position of the antenna and hence disrupt our viewing pleasure.

It was a pretty simple procedure, really. All one had to do was tell Greg that, since the antenna was right outside his window, it was his turn to do it; then, as he turned the apparatus, good old-fashioned communication fine-tuned the operation.

"IS IT GOOD YET?!" was screamed down toward the living room.

"WHAT?" came back, muffled by the corrugated tin roof and the rough-hewn oak frame of the house.

"IS IT GOOD YET?!"

"NO!"

Twist twist twist

"HOW ABOUT NOW?!"

"OKAY – RIGHT THERE... WAIT... GO BACK A BIT... THERE IT... HANG ON BACK THE OTHER WAY JUST A TINY BIT... THERE! PERFECT!"

Then I would dive back in through the window, and tear downstairs where my spot on the couch would now be occupied by one of my idiot brothers or sister and I had to sit on the floor. Which, by the way, also brought with it additional duties, such as being the remote control to turn up the volume or change the channel, and also refill snack bowls and drinks. Kids today have absolutely not Clue One on how easy they have it.

When we tired of, or exhausted, all the American programming, we could watch TV from Montreal, Quebec or Toronto, which consisted of a LOT of hockey, and French Star Trek, plus some decent shows like The Beach Combers and King of Kensington, and tons of BBC programs including our favorite: Monty Python's Flying Circus. So yeah, we were pretty well-rounded with the intercontinental stuff we watched.

AND we learned French by watching the Star Trek episodes we'd already seen a hundred times, and figured out what the French was by extrapolation. We were practically citizens of the world.

Saturday mornings, of course, were holy. Chores were done quickly, if not somewhat incorrectly, so we could drop in front of the TV and watch the cartoons that seemed to last forever. Bugs Bunny/Road Runner hour was a favorite, as were some edgy fringe shows like Under Dog, Rocky and Bullwinkle, and Stop That Pigeon. Jeezum Crow, the feeling one would get from settling in front of HR Puffinstuff with a bowl of Lucky Charms, and if my brother hadn't gotten to it beforehand, a *second* bowl. We were *off the hook*.

This is not to say that we just sat in front of the TV all the time, because we definitely did not. We were very selective about what we watched, and our time was precious; so we planned the watch and watched the plan.

Between the libraries in school and the public library on Main Street 14 miles away, we had plenty to read. There were no banned books; the ones they didn't like, they just didn't carry. And that's why God invented book stores and The Scholastic Book Club. Somehow, we were able to find the good stuff, the Vonneguts, the Hellers, the Hintons and the like. As expected, SE Hinton's books were just the thing for a young boy stuck in a small town, I read them all cover to cover multiple times.

And we still had a shit-ton of time to play outside, and/or do extracurricular activities; from school, scouting, and just general grab-assery. Especially when we were younger, still doing a lot with our father, some of our favorite activities such as hiking, canoeing, fishing and the like, were made extra special by the fact that we got to go places the Normies couldn't go. We'd hike to the top of mountains that held a Fire Tower, and all the tourists had to be content with just looking up at the towers, held at bay by an imposing sign that sternly warned "No Unauthorized Personnel Beyond This Point."

Imagine their jealousy and consternation as we just trotted up with our uniformed Leader, unlocked the chain, and climbed up the staircase to the top. HA HAAAA! Take THAT, suckers! We're Authorized!

We'd get this same feeling in the winter while cross-country skiing, and all the other skiers had to follow the normal trail markers, and stay away from the trails that were similarly designated as NOT FOR YOU. We'd show up, and get to yank that velvet rope aside, and go enjoy Triple Secret Ski Trails that led to magical lands. In reality, these trails usually led to some sort of State-owned/ operated camp, and we had to hang out while our dad investigated, fixed, or locked up a camp that was damaged or left unlocked as that season ended. Was still pretty VIP.

We even on occasion, or at least I know my sister and I, got to go with our mom when she went to visit some clients she helped as a nurse or as some other administrative gig she had. There were some historic and extremely interesting places we got to run around in as Mom worked, The Will Rogers Institute and Land's End to name two.

These cavernous, lumber-based Uber-Great-Camp-type buildings were the things of Haunted Mansion mystery movies. Secret passages, gigantic fireplaces, creaky staircases, musty earthy smells, and angry facilities managers that were older than the building and just as musty-smelling, who "shhhhhh-ed" you as you ran past at top speed, your foot-falls sinking into the carpeting leaving almost no sound, like we were ghosts.

We got to meet some pretty interesting folks this way, and were introduced to a few ideas that we likely would not have had any exposure to for years otherwise: retirement homes, assisted living apartments, hospice care and the like. And of course, we got introduced to the idea of death and funerals. It was all good – for us anyway. Pretty great seeing those places up close and personal.

When we were at school, starting in 6th grade, students were allowed to leave campus and "Go Downtown" during lunch break. It was a short walk down the "highway" into town, or we could go across the pedestrian bridge and take a shortcut through the hillside and show up in the alleys behind the storefronts on Main Street or Broadway.

Magnificent trouble was easy to be gotten into during lunch, and the shit we could do in the space of one hour, holy crap, we should have gotten extra credit bonuses for the time management skills alone, never even mind the multi-tasking.

Feeling punkish? Grab a puff under the highway overpass over the Saranac River. Short on cash? Offer to chop ice out on the stoop of the book store! Don't like work? Try shoplifting at JJ Newberry's, nobody ever watches the candy aisle! And if you like to gamble, the lunch counter at Newberry's had these balloons over the counter where you could pop one and see what you won inside. I won a Banana Split one time. These were not cheapo ones, skimped on because they were free. These were fully loaded splits capable of wiring a child with enough sugar and carbs to fuel some cutting-edge wise-assery for the rest of the day and into the night, if versed in the conservation of energy sciences.

We had a little gang of us that used to do the downtown thing almost every day. One of my best friends, Boyd and his sister, and then a friend of his sister's joined soon after. We knew the Main Street drag like the back of our hands, where to get the best candy, where to sell "antiques" we got from our houses' attics or basements, where the good comic books were and what days the new ones came in, and so forth.

One year we woke up craving criminal behavior, and we did a fair amount of shoplifting; quickly using the gateway drugs of Bubble Yum and Charleston Chews to transition to the hard stuff: small toys.

On some random Fall day, surprise surprise, I had lunch time detention or some such, and could not go with the gang to make the rounds. I was so bummed, we had staked out a particular store that had just gotten some swell small toys in. We had this One Last Job... and then I was OUT.

I got kicked from detention shortly before lunch was over, and saw Boyd sitting on a bench outside the main entrance to the school – he did not look happy.

"Hey man, what we get today?" I asked, kicking brightly-colored leaves up as I approached, wanting to hear everything I'd missed. He didn't even look up, he just let out a quiet sigh and reached into his coat pocket.

When Boyd pulled his hand out, it held a small stuffed animal – one of the ones we'd been eyeing – some sort of precursor to Beanie Babies. He held it out lifelessly on the palm of his hand.

"We got caught," he said dully. "Had to pay for it."

"Damn. That sucks."

And thus ended our life of crime, and none too soon – this impromptu intervention kept us from going down a road that led to one outcome only: a rough stretch of hard time in Dannemora.

Do *sports*, kids... not *crime*.

So yeah, it may seem like there isn't much to do in a small town, but that is misleading and completely subjective. You just got to know where to look, and sometimes be happy with Canadian TV and lunchtime detention. If one is willing to disregard the admonishments and actual rules and laws, the sky's the limit for a child, and many an adult as well.

I'd like to see some of that sort of stuff make it into a Hallmark movie. It would just feel more realistic.

A CASH FLOW THING

Poor. Broke. Destitute. Tight. There are a lot of different terms to describe life without money or high-falutin' material things. And I am sure the degree to which those terms apply change with social norms and mores and whatnot... not to mention personal perceptions as one stands on the different stages that the Theatre of Life makes available.

My wife and I always get into arguments about the meanings of those words and how and when to apply them, and we can never see eye-to-eye; but I don't think either of us really attach too much stigma to whatever version of "no money" our families were at in the past, or where we are at currently. We simply do not agree as to which station we are at, at any given time. I don't even think it matters, but you know, you like to be able to slap a label on temporal circumstances sometimes, like "I can not wait until we have money so we can (insert thing to buy or place to go here)," or "Jesus H Christ I am so sick of being broke all the time."

"We're NOT broke," my wife would say, "we've got it better than *many* other people."

"Yes, and I understand that," I would say, and then snap my mouth shut, sufficing to have used the short-answer in this case.

I have, of course, learned to stuff my long-answer complaints way deep down inside and not voice them, as it just isn't worth it. However, "we *literally* are at the moment," I would *think*, gesturing to the well-designed GUI of our bank account after a particularly debauched and Devil-may-care spree of bill-paying and grocery purchasing. It wasn't an indictment on us as human beings, or our abilities to handle cash, but at this moment in time, because of *reasons*, we were definitionally broke.

Broke ain't poor, and poor ain't destitute. Broke is simply in a state of not having any cash flow; and it can change from day to day.

But anyway, I'm not really sure what we were – financially speaking – as a family when I was a kid in Mohawk Lake. "Chronically low on funds?" Or maybe "intermittently solvent?" I mean I know we didn't have a lot of money; our parents' jobs being what they were – these were not rock-star professions. Even if I had no concept of what a certain job paid and it's standing in the community's hierarchy of judgment, I for sure knew what the tangible realities were. Although I don't think I ever thought of what we were was *poor,* per se.

I was the youngest of four siblings, two brothers and a sister. We had what we needed, but kids tend to notice who has the "nicer" version of things, whether it be book covers, toys, clothes, lunches, or houses. Not that I even cared really. Yeah, would have been nice to have THOSE toys at Christmas, but I quickly got over it. I loved where we lived, and had more than enough fun with what I had, tromping around the woods, splashing around the lake, drawing, writing, taking care of animals and plants, etc.

Everything else was just sort of details that I only recognized after I had grown up and thought back about it.

We shopped for groceries – what we would call the Big Shopping – once a month. That's when we'd get in the station wagon with Mom and hit all the stores for the bulk items: bread, canned or frozen things, boxed foods and such.

Our oldest brother ate a lot. No. No. Not like *you* think "a lot" is. Take whatever it is your brother or Uncle ate that one Thanksgiving which connoted "a lot" to you, and just triple it. My oldest brother would eat an entire box of cereal for breakfast, out of a mixing bowl. He would use an entire loaf of bread to make sandwiches for his lunch when he went to mow lawns. I'm sure if he could have swung it, and they were plentiful, he would have slapped a few pieces of bread on a moose and had that for lunch a few times a week.

You may think, wow what a cow. But he was more like a bull. He was large to begin with, having the gene pool he had, but then he got acquainted at a youngish age with pre-acting-career Arnold Schwarzenegger, and he quickly got himself into a weight-training regimen – on top of all the other work there was to do farm-wise. This alone must have been such a nightmare scenario for a mother of four when it came to food shopping.

This is likely why we shopped where and how we did. We tended to shop at the back of stores and right at the factories. The back of the bakery had all the bread that – while it was not "bad" by any means – was not fresh, the day old, the two days old loaves. It was less expensive, and we bought in bulk, like a lot of families did. Hell, it wasn't going to last long at our house anyway.

In the area we lived there were frozen foods factories/ farms as well, such as Bird's-Eye. If you went directly to the warehouse, you could stock up for way less. Later on, they offered home-delivery and we got that, which saved a drive. Our back-porch freezers were PACKED. To this day I occasionally have dreams about going out on the back porch and opening that one chest freezer to grab a popsicle from the left-hand quarter, which was packed with treats.

For the "regular" once a week shopping, we had two grocery stores to choose from in Saranac Lake: Grand Union or A&P. They were right next to each other on Church Street. If we had money, it was Grand Union, if we were tight, it was A&P and a shit-ton of green and gold stamps and clipped coupons. I always enjoyed pasting those stamps into the books you'd get from the store, it was oddly satisfying.

On the occasions that our dad had a major S&R, or Forest Fire to stomp out, he would get cases and cases of White Rock sodas, and huge boxes of sandwiches from Connor's Inn to feed the crews. If the search ended up rescuing early, or Nature decided to wash away the fire with sky water, Dad'd come home with a lot of those goodies left over – and we'd have over-packed sack lunches for the next week. OH. YEAH.

Sometimes, I guess we were suddenly flush with cash, we did the hour drive to Plattsburgh for the really good grocery stores. With all the left-over money on the way back on those days, we got a special treat for dinner: Kentucky Fried Chicken.

All the groceries we got during the Summer and Fall months went away in the Winter to some extent, as we now had our own stuff put up, so food was never really in short supply.

Clothing was sort of the same, we never really had very little to wear – at least I didn't. I had plenty of hand-me-downs from two brothers. My next oldest brother got some of his from the oldest, and the oldest got a lot of the new stuff. I had a photo of this one shirt my oldest brother wore in the maybe early 70's. Then I had a picture of my next oldest brother wearing it, and then I had a picture of me wearing it in the early 80's. I literally wore it until it fell off my body in college.

At the beginning of the school year, I got my new clothes from the Army/Navy Store or Ames: two new pairs of jeans, a new pair of Converse All-Stars, regular or high-tops, and a new pair of these thick felt liners for my winter boots. Just about everything else was provided by growing brothers who no longer fit theirs.

We had epic sessions just after school started where we would make book covers out of brown paper grocery bags, and then decorate them ourselves. It was all just what we did, I never really felt like "oh we have *this* because we can't afford *that*." And really, 90% of everyone else in the community was about the same; it was not a community of opulence.

We had things until they broke – then we fixed them. If they broke again, we fixed them again. If we couldn't fix them – and there was not a lot we couldn't fix – we found someone who could fix them. We used things until they dissolved in our hands; and *then* we built or bought another one. We broke a lot of bucksaw blades while clearing trails or cutting our own Christmas trees – but we had literal boxes of new blades at our disposal.

I imagine we had quite the credit line at some places, like lumber stores or feed stores. I am pretty certain the animals or the leaky roof did not always wait until our parent's checks cleared the bank. And our father had a lot of side gigs too. He had a landscaping service at one point, which would require a lot of tools, seeds, fertilizers and such to be shipped to our house.

And after that ceased to be – we had a LOT of brand new tools and supplies to use ourselves around the farm. He also had a chimney sweeping company that was short lived. I used to ride my bike around putting his flyers on doors; until I had the brilliant idea to just put them in the mail boxes instead. Man was I clever – why didn't Dad think of that first? Well, because that was technically mail tampering, that's why. Live and learn; and get yelled at.

He also had a side gig sharpening bladed tools like axes and knives, selling shrubs to make hedges out of, and a tool and hardware store that he was working on when I left the house in the late 70s. On that one, he had actually secured a store in Saranac Lake and was in the middle of remodeling it, but it never took off.

Then he had the sheep shed thing, sheered his own sheep, sold the wool at markets or had yarns made from them, then sold the materials and other crafty items with his second wife at a store in Lake Placid. He was pretty damn good at just about anything he tried, I just don't think the market could bear it.

All those side hustles plus the ones I may have forgotten – those ain't cheap. I am sure they did not help with the cash flow situation at all, and his credit rating likely looked like swiss cheese at some point. But you know – we never starved to death or wound up on the street.

So… were we poor when I was a kid? In general? For that specific community? Compared to the National Average? I don't know, not sure I really cared – although knowing what I was like later in life, it clearly affected me a lot. I had a fixation on money – or rather *not* having it – through maybe my 40's.

Sure, we were not swimming in cash when I was a kid, but we figured out how to make things last, and we learned skills necessary to fix, repair or modify. And more importantly, we learned how to do without. I think we just learned the value of things. For me, it was worth it.

It's Who You Know

As an adult, I would volunteer with social programs such as Meals on Wheels and More, Habitat for Humanity, and down at the Austin Resource Center for the Homeless (ARCH) in Austin, TX. I really enjoyed all these programs, where I met a great deal of interesting people.

I especially enjoyed working at the ARCH.

Most people experiencing homelessness get the fast shuffle into a one-size-fits-all category, and this is the very definition of objectification. I had some early experience with homeless folks growing up, and folks who were just having a little extra trouble getting through life, and some that were just plain weird, but got treated differently to some degree for it.

Our small town both accepted and reviled the weird folks in the community, it was sort of strange. I guess most communities are that way, from what I have seen since. It felt like you had to be an exact, specific sort of weird in order to be proudly counted as one of the community. But be the *other* kind or weird… ohhh boy, you're *too* weird. My mom tended to attract that second kind of person a lot; and I will not lie – most of my life has been the same.

My wife will always, without fail, attract folks who just want to open up and tell their life's story, or just chat about their hobbies and work, and significant others, and maybe some issues they are having at the time.

Me? I attract folks who want to tell about the sack of cats they have in their basement, or about the time they had to shave their left leg in order to pull out the weird biohazardous boring beetle that worked its way in when they were cleaning their septic tank. And did I want to see how the hair was growing back. And did I want to see the beetle, cause they haz it in a cigarette box in their pocket.

Frankly it doesn't really bother me much, and it keeps life interesting. I guess my mom probably felt that way when living up there in that small town. She certainly felt the need to bring folks home now and again, whether for a meal, or to talk, or around the holidays when they likely had no other family or friends to go to.

She used to do the same thing when I was a lot older too, in high school and college, when she was an Army recruiter. Sometimes the recruits were joining the Army because they had no place else to go, like Richard Gere's Zack Mayo. And because of that, they had nowhere to go in between when they signed up, and when the bus left the station to take them to Fort Whicheveritwas.

So Mom brought them home.

They'd stay with us for a few days, and then she would drive them to the bus station, and they'd head out to their new lives. Most of them were just normal people on their way to a new chapter, and sadly almost all of them just got lumped into a standard fuzzy memory category in my head. No names, no remarkable features, just a faceless parade.

However, there were a few standouts there, too. I have forgotten their names as well by now, mostly because it's been too many years, but I did use my own proprietary mnemonic device to memorize them to this day. I simply attached a stand-outable fact or event to them, and re-named them according to this event. You know, sort of like the native peoples of this country used to do. For instance:

Ms. Stabs-a-Hand, who really seemed like a nice person for three days, wound up stabbing her bunkmate in the hand with a pair of scissors on her first day at boot camp. One would think this behavior would have made her a shoo-in for Infantry placement or even KP duty, but no, oddly enough it only bestowed upon her a one-way ticket back to her home town, or the town of her choosing.

Mr. Robs-Our-House was a quiet guy who, well, robbed our house after he was done with boot camp. This is a great story too, because he knew where things were from living in our house, so he had planned to come in while everyone was gone, and he knew right where the small combination lock lockbox was kept in the spare room closet.

That was a particularly funny one, because the poor bastard must have spent the whole afternoon working that steel-cased box open with a hammer and a flat-head screwdriver – which I am guessing by the hammer and flat-head screwdriver he left behind after he finished.

The box, much to his surprise – and mine too, really – only contained some baby toys and a bag of rubber bands, which he took with him. Maybe he thought they were special because they were locked away. Maybe he thought he put so much effort into the endeavor, he was getting *something* out of it. Or perhaps he had some demons he was either fighting, or working with (or for), and *they* definitely had use for them. I won't lie, I have no idea why Mom kept baby toys and rubber bands in a steel safe box; but to each, they got their own.

He didn't touch anything else in the house, except for the patio door that he jimmied open. Nice guy, thoughtful; he had a plan, he stuck to it, he eyed the prize, he did no additional harm. I wonder if he had put much thought into just taking the whole box and running? However you sliced it – it was a whole lot of work for nuttin' on his part.

And then there was Ms. Inappropriate Flirt, who I am pretty sure was inappropriately flirting with me on more than one occasion. As she was in her twenties, and I was in my teens still. You might assume that any young high-school-aged male was so full of raging hormones that this was some sort of 80s first-time-sex-romp movie in the making, but no... it was just weird. I excused myself from the room on one really uncomfortable interaction – nothing physical, just a REALLY creepy vibe.

None of these folks ever seemed to mean us any harm, they were just a tad *off* at best, or very specifically task-oriented in their mayhem at worst.

Whatever the case, it gave me a thick skin and an affinity for the type that I never really thought much about over the years, at least not in a good way. When I started to work with folks having a bit of trouble, it felt very familiar, and easy, and eventually I actually felt better talking with "the weirdos" more than I enjoyed talking with "the Normies" that inhabited the rest of my life.

At the ARCH I have had people with absolutely nothing offer me a bite of their sandwich, because they all had one and I didn't. I have walked with a gentleman who was currently homeless because his wife's cancer had wiped them out financially, and when she passed they lost their house.

He was a bioengineering professor, and he was explaining this new process he was working on to make biofuel from seaweed. And every Friday I looked forward to talking to Caroline, who stopped by the center to rest and clean up, and maybe get something to eat at Caritas across the street. She had a wicked, dark sense of humor, and she liked that I did as well. We enjoyed talking to each other, and laughed quite a bit.

There was also a guy we used to call Little Naked Charles Manson, because he looked like a little version of Charles Manson, oh, and the first time I met him he was naked and running from the staff and cops out past the computer lab I was stationed in. He stopped at the doorway, poked his head in and asked with an appropriate sense of urgency "is there a back door out this way?"

pointing toward the door that led to the parking garage. I nodded in affirmation, and he split before I could tell him that the door was always locked. He seemed pretty busy. I'm sure he found out on his own.

When I was a kid in Mohawk Lake, The sort of folks our mom knew and brought to our house, or brought us to them, were similar.

The ancient, nearly skeletal Pete O'Leary, who had lost 1.5 lungs in a horse-riding accident, and constantly had to lug his air around with him in a tank. Pete was some sort of historic figure in Saranac Lake, I never did find out exactly what his deal was there. On occasion, he would use his bed sheets to dress up like a Roman senator when we met him at the door.

There were hippies, and burn-outs, and weirdos and lonely old folks who didn't get out much, and wound up being very socially awkward, perhaps only because they were now talking to a six or seven year old who wasn't much of an actual conversationalist himself... just a *talker.*

I met a folk singer friend of Mom's once as well, I think he worked at a radio station or something. Knowing what I know now, I am pretty sure he was high all the time, and it wasn't on the fresh mountain air that made Saranac Lake famous once upon a time.

Think of any folk-singer you may have seen in any movie or TV show that was making fun of folk singers in the 60s and 70s – that was him. Not saying he was horrible, just typical of that idiom. Eons later, I looked him up – holy cow, he was still doing the folk-singer gig well into his 80s.

But by far, one of my favorite left-of-center people was a guy by the name of Jack Hawkins, or Hawkeye to his friends, such as my mom. Hawkeye lived in a big old antique house, with all kinds of really old cars dotting the parcel of land. I am pretty sure he either used to be or still was a mechanic by trade.

He raised some animals I think, or at least he had them wandering around on his property, and I know for a fact that he had this wild chicken, or grouse or the like that he literally raised from an egg he found in the woods. This was his buddy, and it ran around his equally antique-stuffed house – which had no running water, no insulation, and no central heat – without concern.

He had old weapons from the Civil War, he had a potbellied stove in the kitchen that he cooked on, wooden barrels that collected rainwater, and gardens for vegetables. He was often seen driving any number of his old vehicles around on the roads, and any time our car would have to reduce speed all the sudden when driving home because of backed-up traffic, it was likely because Hawkeye was just ahead, doing the top speed of his 60-year-old Model T which was about 20mph.

He would stop by our house frequently while driving one of his old cars, and as kids we loved it. We'd hear the AAAAA-oooooo-GAAAA of his klaxon, and rush out to see what he was driving this time. In the winter, he wore a huge fur car coat that looks like it was made out of the skins of three bears and a couple wolves, and he smoked a corncob pipe. He frequently wore driving goggles, as his cars rarely had windshields. This was my kind of guy, he was total weird in the right way.

Sadly, he stopped coming by after an altercation with our old man one Christmas. I watched from the window as he intercepted Hawkeye before he could pull into our driveway in his stripped down 1923 American-LaFrance fire truck. I could barely make out Dad's dulcet tones thundering out a friendly (sarcasm) hello, and clearly saw the wide smile of Hawkeye as he waved in reply, more than half in the bag. Dad knocked Hawkeye's hand aside and pointed in the direction of the road that he would prefer Hawkeye continue travelling in.

Not sure why Dad would allow him to drive home drunk, but at 20 mph, he likely wasn't going to hurt anyone but himself; especially in winter when the roads were flanked by four-foot-high snowbanks like bowling alley bumper rails.

Hawkeye made a vague hand gesture of contrition, patted the spare riding quilt on the passenger-side bench seat, and pulled another beer out from beneath it. Both the single, and the rest of the sixer under that blanket were confiscated with prejudice from the fire truck, and then the direction Hawkeye was to navigate was re-emphasized with more vigor. This time the truck putted off. He never visited our house again, and any time we saw him after that was a stolen trip to his weathered, unpainted home.

I learned just a few years ago that Hawkeye had passed away at the age of 83 or some such amount, and left quite a legacy of old cars and trucks that were in really great shape. I wish I had kept up with him over the years, would have loved to help him fix up a car or two when I was grown and living back there. I knew where to find him, but I never stayed in touch.

Keeping in touch would have been tough, by today's standards – I would have had to write letters by hand, and I was never great at that much. Even with the advent of email, and if he had electric power, I know he would have never had a computer or internet.

I recall talking with my mother shortly after Hawkeye passed, and she said "Did I ever tell you about his previous life, before I met him?"

She had met him, as she did a lot of folks at that time, when she was helping care for him when he was quite ill, as he had no close family in the area. The reason he had no close family in the area was because he had pretty much cut off ties with them when he was younger, and moved to this middle-of-nowhere location. His family, apparently, had started some tool company on one side, and a ceramics company on the other. They were wealthy – as Chris Rock would say – "I'm not talking 'bout rich, I'm talking 'bout wealthy," like Stupid Money wealthy.

At some point early on, he renounced that wealth, and actually never wanted, nor asked, for any of it. Never really traded on the family name much, apparently. I have never knowingly met too many people like that, that walked that particular talk. But he did. He was happy with his land, his cars, his poetry, and piano. And beer.

He was an original, a hold-over from a different time, larger than life, a stand-out among the class... and definitely a memorable person to know as a kid.

I WOULD NOT DIE OUT IN THE WOODS

Dad tried to kill us many times. I'm not saying we didn't deserve it every single time, because I'll just bet we did. But it happened. I literally have lost track of the exact number of times, and with most of those, it was just The Look that did it. Deep in my heart I know without a doubt that the reason The Look failed to do us in properly every time, was because Dad had not yet consumed enough human souls.

Our father was an imposing guy, the grandson of a Russian blacksmith. Even though he was an inch or so shorter than our grandfather at six feet tall, he carried himself like he was 9 foot 3 and made out of iron, with flaming black holes for eyes, and powder keg for a voice. For all the humor that he had, and all the good qualities he possessed, he was also a natural prodigy in the ways of harm both physical and mental, and he often wielded both at the same time, although he maybe didn't know it.

When we did something "bad," his punishment was swift and ouchfull; he'd grab whatever he could lift and introduce it to our asses – and he could lift a LOT. His two favorite items to whack us with were his belt, and this shillelagh he had gotten while in Ireland during his Navy days. A shillelagh, for those of you who do not speak the language, is Irelandish for "half a tree."

This half a tree was the kind they sold in gift shops, I imagine. Polished and lacquered shiny, it had a bright green shamrock emblazoned on it, and quite frankly, I wish I still had it hanging on the wall, just because. When we were kids, it hung on a nail from a rafter in attic. Just at the top of the stairs. When it was clobberin' time, not only did we have the fear of the physical damage we were about to have, but to make matters worse, he would send the offending child – usually me – up into the attic to fetch the item of ass-swellification.

The attic, in this 108-year-old (at the time) house, was the stuff of nightmares, and matched in its horror only by the cellar. Both had a rich darkness that could only be formed by the complete and utter lack of light and hope, and an air so thick with malice and doom, you could cut a slice of it, toast it, and butter it with your own fear and dread.

The only saving graces of the attic were A) it had windows, so at least it was well lit in the daytime, and B) the fact that when outrunning the demons, ghosts and monsters that dwelled there, you could build up momentum because it was all downhill to the exit.

In the basement, it was *always* pitch black. You had to turn off the light, then run through the waist-deep quicksand that was the upward flight of 27 creaky wooden stairs with no hand rails.

When sentenced to obtain Captain Ass-Cracker in the attic, however, one would walk as slow as possible upon exit, if only to give the Dark Ones their shot and absorbing us first, and denying Dad the pleasure.

But the single most terrifying thing our father ever did to us, when we did something bad, was to NOT be home when we did it. When he was home, and we, say, kicked a hole in the brand new aluminum screen door, it was swift and easy corporal punishment. The equation looked something like this:

> *destruction of property + proximity to Dad*
> *= immediate comeuppance.*

But when we did something naughty – let's just say for the sake of this writing, that somehow we boys had taken it into our heads to knock icicles off the edge of the roofs with snowballs we threw at them, being scientific about the endeavor by seeing that only a very specific density and weight of snow-ball was enough to break those icicles, and once we had achieved that density/ weight recipe, employed it at our discretion and delight so much so that one of us did not notice that behind those icicles there were house windows with a certain dollar value attached to them, and that after an icicle or three was gone it left a gap where, in theory, the next dense/ heavy snowball could easily pass through leaving the remaining icicles unscathed, but the window pane – in the middle of winter – not so lucky – AND Dad was NOT home, well, it did this:

It created a time/pain vortex in our lives.

I know my older brother and I once tried to come up with a name for it, that time in between when we did the thing, and when we knew our father would be home and notice it. Hitchcock had it right, you didn't need to see the murder on screen, you just needed to anticipate it, and know its presence was imminent to be mortified by it. And that period of time, between transgression and justice, was the worst feeling in the world.

Oh the things we imagined. We knew what he was capable of, and the thoughts of it were still worse. What would it be? The Voice? That bellowing that had been known to broil trout in the lake 100 yards away? The Look? Which was the only known thing to stop a charging Adirondack black bear in its tracks? Or The Item of Fate, that would be chosen completely at random from whatever was nearby when he noticed the Thing We Did. An item such as a tree, an old car engine, or even one of the other children? If Mercury was in retrograde, it was usually all three. Mercury Psssshhh. What a dick planet.

Anyway, the point is, Dad was able to mete out the punishment in such a fashion you really would have thought we would have learned how to NOT fuck things up in a punishable way, or at least not get caught. But sometimes it was that very fear that helped us live.

One winter in particular, I was playing my favorite game of "Let's see how far back in the woods I can go in the middle of winter, and not die." The game was a LOT of fun, and had pretty simple rules: 1) see how far you can go back into the woods in the middle of winter, and 2) don't die. Sound pretty innocuous? See, that's where you'd be wrong, because if you grew up in that neck of the woods and had the Adirondacks as your playground, and were also blissfully unaware of the dangers that await you out there... it could prove to be The Most Dangerous Game, indeed.

I LOVED tromping around in the woods, ESPECIALLY in the winter. All that snow, all those trees, all those trees covered in snow. It was a magic world, full of branches to shake snow off of, cold trees with brittle branches to climb, snow covered boulders to climb and jump off of into more snow, and some sort of large animal tracks that looked pretty fresh to follow deeper into the woods while it was snowing.

On this specific occasion, I was engaged in the fulfilling practice of every one of the above activities, when at one point I looked up and noticed it had started to snow significantly harder than before, covering up my tracks which I could have followed home. Oh, and also it was getting dark. Would not have been such a bad thing, though, cause if you told someone where you were going "to play" they could come find you when you didn't return.

By the way, I never really told anyone where I was going when I went out to play, unless I was going somewhere on my bike. Like it would have mattered anyway...

I mean, it was a HUGE "backyard," what was I supposed to say "I'll be by the tree that is next to that other tree, over where all the trees are?" You die out *there*, it becomes a dental-records-five-years-from-now issue.

On this late winter afternoon, I was going to die by simply being dumb. My body would freeze solider than a block of ice in these temperatures, probably as my numbing hands shook the last of the snow off some beautiful fir tree.

It wouldn't be long before some large animal that was being followed caught wind of me, managed to circle back, and found me and then got annoyed that it had to chew so hard because I was freezing, causing it to shake me like a rag doll and throw me over a cliff in anger. My body would careen off outcroppings and tree stumps on the way down that cliff face, landing with a loud KRACK as all my limbs were forced in varying directions in all three dimensions on the X, Y, and Z axes.

And then, *then,* the worst would happen: Dad would get home.

He'd wonder where the hell that no good son of his was, and he'd have to call a search and rescue party made up of the finest forest rangers employed by the New York State Department of Environmental Conservation, and they'd use their famous Grid Search method, famously known for finding car keys dropped in a meadow. In this case the car keys would be my now solid-frozen body at the bottom of a granite cliff, with a broken Large Animal fang stuck in my eye and a snowless fir tree branch clutched in one stupid hand.

And Dad would be PISSED.

He would be FURIOUS. He would literally use his special DEC-ordained bring-them-back-to-life powers to bring me back to life, force me to do my chores (as well as everyone else's chores in the house) while he yelled at me the whole time.

Then he would brow-beat me for three days, by *actually* beating me with his eye-brows, and finally he would make me give a public apology on the school bus where I would have to state what I had done to embarrass him in the community; and then, and only then, he would release me from my earthly form and absorb my soul to make him stronger than ever.

And it was the thought of THAT, and only that, which gave me the strength to find a landmark or two and be able to triangulate where the Hell I was and waddle through the waist-high snow back to the house, and NOT die out in the woods in the middle of winter.

THE ALBANY BUS STATION INCIDENT

When I was in fourth grade, my parents divorced. Or maybe just started the separation process. Whatever the deal, my mother moved out of the house with my sister and next oldest brother. They still lived in town, in fact right across from the middle school I attended. Sometimes I would go over after school, sometimes stay the night or weekend. It was – for what it was – kinda nifty having another "home" to go hang out at; like having a fort out in the woods where you could go to turn off whatever flavor of bullshit was happening in your "real" house.

Not entirely sure why I chose (or maybe was chosen) to stay in my father's house when they separated – very likely it was a simple matter of fear of change. I was afraid of everything when I was a kid, so let's go with that scenario.

Within a year – it feels like – my brother moved back into Dad's house, and my mother chose to move away from the idyllic setting that had been her home. She went downstate to Glens Falls, she met a man there, they moved in together, eventually got married, and then moved to Albany at some point.

This movement allowed me a few things more than just the fort out in the woods, which was now farther away. It allowed me to sort of G. Gordon Liddy some of my other fears, such as travelling alone, meeting new people, and figuring out for myself how to navigate in the altogether unfamiliar world of another city, which for many intents and purposes could have been another planet.

The bus ride to Glens Falls wasn't bad, a few hours on an Adirondack Trailways Bus to a niceish bus station in a niceish little Adirondack village. I learned to actually enjoy the three hour ride, meandering through the quaint little villages on the way south. I even managed to talk with fellow riders on occasion, as long as they started the conversation first.

One of my most memorable conversations was with a college student, I think he was a grad student, who was studying in the field of Geology. He introduced me to the concept of Plate Tectonics, and continental shift when I was what, maybe 10 years old. He liked to talk, he seemed pretty damn smart to me, and he answered my somewhat ignorant questions like I was an adult, which I found to be a rather nice change.

He got off the bus a few stops before Glens Falls, and once again I was left to stare out the window, keeping to myself until I arrived at the station, where my mom was always waiting.

The bus stations at all the stops between Saranac Lake and Glens Falls were pretty similar – no real, stand-alone station, but rather stops outside bookstores, novelty shops and drugstores. You'd get your tickets at the counter inside, and then just wait outside on the sidewalk until the appointed time. If you had a longer wait, there were usually diners right next door, or some shop to spend the time in.

This one year, I was a bit older – newly teen-aged I think – and used to the bus trips; I had returned home a bit early. No one was there to greet me as I stepped off the bus out front of the small drugstore on Broadway, just a few doors down from the Pontiac theater. I did what seemed to be my MO: I started to walk. It was Sunday, most of the stores were closed either for Sunday reasons or for early o'clock reasons, so I couldn't go inside the drugstore to use the pay phone and my trusty bag of change. In all reality, I could have walked all the way home, it was only about 13 miles away. I might have tried that, had one building not gotten in my way a short walk down the street: the bowling alley.

I knew this bowling alley, they had bowling in there. But they also had this new stand-up game console inside that was a sort of novelty – us kids had discovered it during a lunch-hour run into town: Brickout. I called my house, no answer. Then I called my grandparents' house, got my grandmother on the phone, told her the situation.

She said she'd call to get Dad or his new wife to pick me up, or at the very least, Grandpa would come get me, to just wait where I was. By the way – where was I calling from?

"I'm at the bowling alley, Grandma." I said matter of factly, "the bus stop was closed."

My grandmother immediately adopted an urgency in her voice, "DON'T YOU GO INSIDE THE BOWLING ALLEY," she warned, "YOU STAY OUTSIDE UNTIL WE PICK YOU UP!"

"I will, grandma, the pay phone is outside." And I hung up.

The pay phone was inside. I was inside. In point of fact, I had been eyeing the Brickout game the whole time. I knew how long it took to drive from our house to town, I had a bag of quarters, I was going to get some high score action.

The funny thing was, even at that age, I wondered why Grandma was so insistent that I not enter the den of iniquity that was the local bowling alley. What horrors did she think were there that awaited me? I knew my father and grandfather would bowl often enough, and I knew my grandmother went with them a time or two, so what was so bad? She sounded pretty adamant that I not go in, because likely I would never return.

In my mind grew moving images of my grandparents fighting along side my father as they battled the bowling-shirted army of darkness that made up the demographic of the family fun center inhabitants. Why would they go there so often if it meant having to bop their way out?

I respected my grandmother, and wanted to make sure she didn't worry about me; but I found it just a *tiny* bit amusing that the bowling alley was, in her mind, the apex of dangerous places for a kid to hang out. But I also really wanted to play that game. And besides, after what happened in what we now refer to as the "Albany Bus Station Incident," I was a seasoned pro at this.

When my mother moved farther downstate, to the Capital, the ride time almost doubled, it was now a five-hour ride one-way. I was 11-ish, but was still not very comfortable nor pulled-together being on my own out among the English; not like future me, who walked boldly into bowling alleys on a Sunday morning in a town whose population was nearly 5,000.

The Albany bus station? Fuuuuuuck. THIS was BUS STATION. Way bigger, and way more diverse than the drugstores I was used to; which meant – to me – way more frightening. I can't even imagine what I would have done were I ever to have to go to a New York City station. But, luckily for me, as always, my mother was there to meet me almost as soon as I stepped of the Greyhound bus. So I had that.

Except for that one time she didn't.

Nor did her new husband.

On this one trip, when I was probably 11 or 12 years old or so, I got off the bus to be greeted only by the unconcerned glances of fellow travelers as they went about their own business in the station. No one really seemed to notice the anxiety I was having at really being alone in the "Big City." (In point of fact, in 1976 the population of

Albany was roughly 500,000; which was around the same population of Austin, TX when we moved there in 1991.)

Mind you this was a good twenty years before cell phones were widely available, so there was no instant access to who you needed – but they had these things on the walls where you clinked coins into the box and you could use a phone. There was usually maybe one or two of these "pay phones" that worked, out of a bank of ten.

Luckily, I had a little baggie of coins for this reason; I found a phone that worked, very careful to check all the others for abandoned change in their coin returns, so at least maybe I could make some cash on the deal. I called Mom's place, let her know I was in, and was told something similar to "oh geez, I lost track of time I will be there as soon as I can. Just stay where you are."

Just stay where I am. I was a master at that. So, I clutched my little suitcase, proceeded to move from where I was, and take a look around. I watched folks hurry to or from other busses, watched folks get information from the kiosk, go in and out of the bathrooms, meet their loved ones. Likely, one or two made some drug deals or kidnapped complete strangers... I never would have known what I was looking at.

But one thing seemed to attract my attention more than others, and that was the blinding shard of sunlight that stabbed through a windowless door at the back of the room as people went in and out.

Oh... sunlight, air... I could do that, I thought. I was vaguely familiar with those things. How could sunlight and air possibly ever steer me wrong? Maybe I could go wait to be picked up out there? Had Future Greg been available at that time, I might have had some insight as to my decision-making, something like:

"You want to get abducted and never seen again? Cause THAT is how you get abducted and never seen again."

Armed with the complete and utter ignorance that was mine in spades, I walked over and opened the door and stepped just outside the threshold, blinked a few times to adjust to the light of the mid-day sun. As the heavy, solid metal door clanked shut behind me, I noticed some very specific imagery that has stuck with me for years.

About four or five people, might have all been men, were standing around smoking cigarettes in the alley behind the bus station. All of whom looked like they had answered the ad

"Wanted: someone to abduct young kids and make them never be seen again."

If you have ever seen a city bus station before, or have any sort of pre-conceived ideas about what they might look like, lower the bar a few seven notches, and you have the "smoking area" in the alley behind the bus station in almost any major city. Dumpsters, large plastic bags leaking goo, pallets, ebola.

Now the folks that were there, in all fairness, were very likely not all that bad – unless they were viewed in the eyes of a young boy who grew up on a farm out in the BFE and did not travel much. The tattoos, the piercings, the cigarettes, the coarse language, ill-fitting clothes, slacky attitudes and postures; one would think they all just got out of prison. In point of fact, I am only sure that the one guy who was closest to me had actually just gotten out of prison.

I know this because he told me.

This guy was probably late thirties, early forties, skinny as a rail, bad haircut, tats up both arms, twitchy kind of look. One hand thumb-hooked to his pocket, the other working that cigarette. He side-eyes me as soon as I walk out, chins me hello.

"Hey kid. Want a cigarette?"

I nod back, then shake my head no. I clearly have walked into the middle of a conversation that was above my pay grade, and clearly out of my wheelhouse. But this guy, for some reason, saw in me someone who needed some life advice from someone who had clearly made poor life choices on more than one occasion.

He took a long drag from his cig, then had some words with his compatriots, they all seemed to agree on whatever it was he talked about. Then he looked at me and said something akin to "listen to me – make sure you never go to prison, kid. You do not want to know the kind of shit you see in prison."

I nodded my head as if I understood, which I kind of did. I looked at the other members of this zigaretteklatsch, they nodded in solemn agreement, Marlboros frozen almost to their lips as they stared into a meaningful space in the distance. I looked back at the Leader, he took another drag, blew it out.

"I was in for five years, I just got out three days ago. I seen some shit in there, man, and learned some shit that I never thought I'd learn."

He got a weird look in his eye, then, with his left palm facing upward, he made a kinda gnarled peace sign and pointed it directly at my throat just under my chin, the fingertips just ever so slightly grazing the skin.

"I could kill you with two fingers, and nobody would ever know what happened to you." He immediately retracted his teaching hand, jammed it in his pocket, took a really long drag on the cigarette, and held it for a while. His friends just nodded, yeah, man… they knew. And now I knew.

"Don't get sent to prison, kid." Were his final words.

What I knew was limited in its scope, but I was certain of this: the little slice-of-life lesson had one of two reasons behind it. A) He meant it; he really was trying his best to keep another wayward kid from ending up in The Joint and ruining their life. I felt this one was the real one – which I triangulated from the looks on the other people's faces. It felt sincere. Earnest.

The B) reason was also a possibility; however, feel I will never know if it was the right one, and through the years I have always hoped that it was *not* the one:

He was totally fucking with me. His buddies were in on it, snickering and chuckling, fist-bumping before it became a thing after the whole slap-me-five jive of the 70's faded to legend.

Ultimately, it didn't really matter much which it was, my reaction was the same: I nodded, scanned the folks once more, reached back to the door handle without taking my eyes off the Leader, and backed my way into the station again.

Found my mom eventually, had a good weekend, returned to my little village in the northern Adirondacks – and never did anything (or maybe just never got caught doing anything) that resulted in me getting sent to prison.

Thank you, Bus Station Back Ally Cigarette Prison Guy. Your rough-and-tumble life choices and experience were not all in vain, you helped a kid you didn't even know lead a good life. That's gotta be some sort of karma banked for your account, and was something I didn't even know I needed at the time.

MOHAWK LAKE

Mohawk Lake; a beautiful little puddle surrounded by trees and mountains in upstate New York, is such a gorgeous, fantastic body of water. It isn't as big as many of the lakes nearby, but it has charm by the packbasketful. Flanked on three sides by St. Regis Mountain, Seward Mountain and McKenzie and Whiteface Mountains, the views are insane. There was never a time of year where you would look outside, blow a raspberry, and say "Oh, *this* fuckin' garbage again."

You wouldn't like it, though, so don't even bother visiting. Nothing to see. Forget I mentioned it.

Unlike many of the lakes and ponds up in that area, Mohawk Lake had just the one iteration; there was no "Upper" or "Middle" or "Lower" as with the Saranac Lakes. Though years before we lived there, it was called

Big Mohawk... in order to differentiate it from Little Mohawk, a stone's throw to the west. The funny thing is, Little Mohawk still exists; I guess at one point in the Town Meeting the leaders just threw up their hands and decided on the simpler "Mohawk Lake."

Good call, I mean otherwise, at some point, every body of water would have "Medium," and "Inverse," and "Not Quite As Big As" modifiers, making the area a living nightmare for Adirondack Guides. Can you imagine the blowback, in 1887, when Ol' Frank Hobart accidentally took his hunting party to "Left-Hand Collier Pond" instead of the contracted "Juxtaposed Collier Pond" like he was supposed to? Bedlam.

Anyway.

Way back in the before times, 1960s-70s – that lake was my JAM. So much to do for a young boy with a lot of imagination and questionably low common sense. Much of my down-time as a misspent youth was misspented by, on, or in that lake. Fishing, swimming, crawfish hunting, baby catfish catching, nearly drowning, and playing Huckleberry Finn on the occasional floating dock section that worked its way loose from some neighbor's beach front and found its way down to me.

Bobbers and worms were like crack to me. I know, I know, A River Runs Through It-styled fly fishing, or even cast-n-crank lure-tugging is for true connoisseurs, but for my money – which was pretty much non-existent – give me a bobber and a can of worms. I'd sit on the dock attached at the front of the boat house all day long on any given Sunday, just drowning worms from late in the morning until the sun went down behind the tower on St. Regis Mountain.

I'd cast that line out as far as I could, standing on tip toes as the line went zipping out of the open-faced reel, to maximize the distance. Then I'd just stand or sit, and watch as the bobber lazily bobbed its way from east to west, or the other which around depending on the wind, and then I'd have to reel it back in and start over again.

Often, the happy, soothing bobberating was rudely interrupted by some dick-bag fish who happened to find the Inquisitioned worm, and then I'd have to reel it in early, deal with the rainbow trout, or largemouth bass, or useless perch, or absolutely no-reason-for-living sunfish before continuing on with my water/bobber activities.

Sometimes, if I dozed a bit, the wind/waves blew that line over into the weeds off to the east of the dock, and the hook-shaped worm would sink to the bottom and get glorped up by a catfish. Catfish don't fight much if they are not challenged for a password upon glorping a worm. To them, they just had a snack; and since there was no yank-back from me, the cat would just sit there quietly enjoying the aftertaste. I'd inevitably notice where the bobber was at some point, start reeling what I thought was an empty line in, when YOINK, that cat would object to my actions and start a campaign to remain where it was. I didn't mind the over-reacting on their part, they were a fun and exciting catch.

I was nearly always smarter than any fish in THAT lake. I ate a lot of trout, and bass and catfish. I didn't have to worry much about eating *all* the fish in the lake though. As luck would have it, a mile or two down the road was the DEC Fish Hatchery, a very interesting and educational place where one could see the life of a fish from eggs to 20-inch Rainbow Trout.

Then, if we were lucky, we'd be sitting down on the dock fishing, or maybe swimming, when we'd hear the chopper. The state helicopter came in low over the lake from the west, and started unloading fish via its belly doors to restock the lake. I just knew that if I cast my line in that direction, I'd get that 20-inch sucker. Yeah, it didn't really work like that. But a kid could dream.

We got ducks at one point too, a gaggle of them. We got the hatchlings in the spring, raised them up in the barn till they got bigger, featherier, and quackier, and then had an epic Moses-Leading-The-Ducks-To-The-Promised-Lake moment when we herded them down out of the barn to the water. Our dog even helped steer them, it was really fun. About two thirds of the way down, those ducks caught the scent of the lake, and they took off like bats who also wanted to go to the lake.

Other, wilder, aquatic birds would visit as well. One late afternoon when I was still casting as the sun was going down. I heard a loud splash off to my left. I look over and this HUGE Great Blue Heron was standing maybe six feet from me in the shallow water getting a drink. Even with it standing in the water and me on the dock, it still looked like it was taller than me. It never even acknowledged my existence, just gulped some more water, then took off again. NOICE.

There was some sort of summer camp directly across the lake from our stretch of beach, I believe it was a Girl Scout Camp. On more than one occasion, I would get down to the boat house to fish, and when the doors swung open out onto the dock, I was greeted by the sight of a bunch of girls roughly my age, sunning themselves on our floating dock.

Bit of a surprise the first time, a highly anticipated event afterward. Seems to earn their swimming badge, at some point the ladies had to swim across the lake and back, and they would rest once they made the first trip. I can not vouch for how cool I was while trying not to look like a little nerd fishing; but I am pretty sure I came across as a little nerd fishing. Ahhhh, summer.

Winter brought a different sort of fun to Mohawk Lake. Yeah, it was cold as shit, and the lake was now covered by (I hoped) a foot or more of solid ice, but there was shit that needed doing. Shoveling off a large patch of ice to skate on, or drilling a hole to ice fish with my highly illegal tip-up rig, which ironically was provided by my father whose job it was to ticket or arrest folks who used illegal tip-up rigs.

Sometimes, mother nature would help a brother out, and the wind would strip the snow off the ice for quite a distance on the lake front. When that happened, I – not being the strongest of ice skaters – would lace-up the skates, stand in one spot with my back to the wind, and then open my coat out to the sides like a sail, and just ride the wind until I stopped somewhere down the shoreline. The real bitch was trying to skate against that same wind to get back.

But the absolute best was the snowmobiling. In small towns such as where I grew up, snowmobiling was God's answer to "what do I do when I can't drive my car in the snow, but I still want to be involved in some sort of vehicular wreck, occasionally also involving alcohol?" I was a kid, so I just enjoyed the wind in my face aspects of skidooing on the lake, notsomuch the drinking.

I will admit, to this day, I still try to imagine what the count is now for snow mobiles at the bottom of the lake, you know from those times when someone was inclined to both fuck around AND find out "if the lake ice is thick enough yet (or still)."

To this day I still have dreams that I am canoeing, kayaking, swimming or even flying around that lake, and when I wake up, I start to think about all the great times I had there again.

Best lake on the face of the planet. But it doesn't really exist, so no point in going to visit. I mean that. Don't even bother.

MY FRIEND WALTER

From my very first day of school — kindergarten at Mohawk Lake Elementary — I could tell I was not built for the standard organized education experience. And indeed, by the time I graduated college nearly 45 years later via an online college program, I was proven correct.

The kindergarten teacher was a short, round, angry and joyless woman by the name of Mrs. Rathbone. As I get older, her face and exact words start to finally fade from my memory, but I will never forget the way she made me feel, or her actions.

On the first day of school, we students were instructed to sit in a circle so that we could share in whatever nurturing experience was about to happen. Perhaps a rousing game of Duck, Duck, Goose, or an exhilarating, blood-pounding round of Roll The Ball to Someone You Do

Not Know and Say 'I would like to meet..." Whatever the activity, I was not feeling it so much. I sat at my tiny little metal desk, content to watch from a safe distance; I mean I hardly knew these people. What if they had cooties?

Mrs. Rathbone invited me to join my new friends.

No thank you, I likely replied politely.

No, seriously, this is a fun way to get to know each other, she insisted.

I am good, really, but thank you for your generous offe...

GAHHHHH, a thick, meaty hand clamped down on my shoulder, as stern, yet unfriendly Mrs. Rathbone gently guided me from my sitting position to a somewhat standing position (It was not so much a standing position as it was a hanging from a meat hook sort of situation).

As you might imagine, I was a bit taken aback, and I may have resisted, no matter how futile. This resistance was met with – and I shit you not – the business end of one of her swollen, support-hosed legs kicking me in my ass as she jerked me toward the circle of initiates who just sat there and watched in horror.

A few more kicks and jerks got me to my spot, at which time I was unceremoniously dropped like a filled diaper into my tiny arc of the circle to participate in the fun and educational ice-breaker game she had lovingly planned for us five-year-olds (I was 4 and a half, but who's counting). If those other 15 kids didn't know who I was up to this point, they sure as shit knew now. Ice broken. Lifelong school expectations set.

As one might be able to infer, there wasn't much room in a very small town for those people who are, shall we say, a tad to the left or right on the Normal Scale. Normal being as subjective as it is, still has a meaning within any community, and the smaller the community, the more they like to keep that needle where it belongs. Even when it is unintentional; the non-normalness, that is. To put a finer point on that, there is a difference between being a somewhat eccentric artist *non-normal*, and being someone with actual physical or psychological issues or needs *non-normal*.

There was a family that lived in our area, and they had a daughter. To us boys in that hamlet, this young woman was pretty attractive, and we may or may not have thought about her once or twice and maybe even taken notice when she was seen out walking. I think she was fairly close to my oldest brother's age, she certainly wasn't very close to mine.

A time or two, when she was sitting on a rock down at the Mohawk Lake outlet enjoying the weather, and I happened to be fishing there, I would say hello, we chatted briefly, nothing major, but she seemed pleasant enough. Knowing what I know now, I get the feeling that she may have just been lost in those thoughts that one gets when they are now out of high school and realize that the world awaits them – now all they have to do is decide which world they want to hang out in, this small town, or somewhere out *there*.

One day, I heard my father talking with someone – I cannot recall who he was talking to, either there in person or on the phone, but he kept mentioning "that retarded girl who lived nearby." I sat there, screwing up my face, trying to get my brain to think like a grown up, but for the life of me I could not think of who he was talking about. I knew what retarded meant – it was a different time in a much different place – so I had a picture in my head of what I thought this person might look or act like. Mind you, the word instantly brought up images in the mind, and the images were not friendly ones.

Nothing.

His conversation lasted a good five minutes more, within which time "the retarded girl" was mentioned a few more times. I gave up. Then, for whatever reason, something got said on the other side, and my father elaborated on her a bit, and in that sentence I knew exactly who he was talking about.

Not being particularly worldly or well read, I had not met or dealt with many people at that point in my life, but I felt like I knew people somewhat, especially people closer to my age than my father's age. Whatever the case, the young woman was not – in my humble opinion – what he'd been calling her. She simply was not built for a very small town's judgement of what a normal girl should act like. The older I got the more that behavior and thought bothered me, once I knew all the shorthand and metaphorical speech.

Man, if they talked that way about someone who just didn't care about the norms that were expected, how did they talk about the kids that rode our school bus that did indeed actually have some sort of physical or mental difference of ability? And then I thought, much later in life of course, of just how difficult it must have been for those with "alternative lifestyles" to live in a community like that, in the late 60s and 70s.

And worse yet than having to hide a lifestyle or preference from the world, I thought about those who had some sort of difference of ability or imagined lifestyle *thrust* upon them, and were labeled, and dismissed, or marginalized for a good portion of their lives simply because the good folks of this community didn't know how to diagnose or treat, or even just simply behave around them.

My mother, in general a caring person, and a bit of a self-admitted "acquired taste," always seemed to attract a certain element in any community where she lived and worked. Even in tiny little Saranac Lake and the surrounding areas she found them: folks experiencing homelessness, people having a lot of troubles, eccentrics, hippies, weirdos, and forgotten people. She'd go to where they were to help, she'd bring them home to have a meal and a small Christmas present. Stuff I never really thought about too much, except, as a child, that it inconvenienced me somewhat because it took focus off me and my needs.

But these were just normal people having normal human issues, and my mother cared enough to help in any way she could. And I think it was one of the things that acted as a wedge between her and our father and community in general.

From Kindergarten through third grade, I had a friend named Walter. Walter looked a lot like me, we got along great we hung out together on the playground, we talked a lot – he seemed like a perfectly normal kid to me. At recess I would wait at the end of the building of the elementary school near the swings and the merry go round, until I saw him come running out of the doors toward me.

One day he didn't. I knew he was in school, I had seen him in class that morning, so why did he not come out to play? When class was back, I had to go use the bathroom at some point, so I got the hall pass and walked down toward the restrooms. On the way, I passed the office of some teacher or school official, I think, in hindsight it may have been the nurse's office. And there inside was Walter, lying on the bench with a damp rag on his forehead, crying and the nurse talking quietly to him.

I heard later that Walter's grandfather had died suddenly that morning, and Walter was inconsolable after that. He was never quite the same, never ran as fast, never seemed to smile anymore; and then one day he wasn't even in class again. Nobody said anything about why. From fourth through eighth grade I never saw Walter again, never heard anything about him either. Until one day in high school, I was talking with a friend during lunch.

The subject came up about kids we used to know that weren't in our classes anymore, and I mentioned Walter. My friend looked at me and said,

"I know him, he's been in Special Ed for years. You didn't know that?"

Special Ed, of course, being the program for students with physical and mental disabilities that precluded them from participating in the rest of the classes all the other students attended. Or at least they didn't have the same classes all the time, like maybe only one day a week.

If I had thought anything about what happened to him, I may have thought that perhaps he had moved away; it had happened a lot. Hell, I was one of those kids who "just moved away" later that year.

My friend then took me inside to the classroom for Special Ed and showed me the class picture that was hanging on the wall. There, in the back row, was Walter.

I think I literally just blinked for a minute or two. Wow. "Special Ed?" He was a normal kid, he was a friend of mine at one point, surely I would have noticed. Wouldn't I? He looked awful. Sullen look on his face, lifeless, sad. I had no idea what to say or do.

But then it hit me as I looked at the others in the class photo. There were two other kids there that I sort of knew, they weren't really friends, but I had talked with them before – they were actually just kind of rebels and punks, but it NEVER occurred to me they were "Special Ed" material.

A few of the other kids I also knew, one rode our bus – they actually did have special needs. When I was older it occurred to me that "Special Ed" may have just been the legendary kitchen "junk drawer" where things got shoved when you quickly could not think of what to do with them, but you also couldn't justify throwing them away just yet.

Now, I have no illusions, I am not an expert, nor a trained professional, but I have had conversations with at least three of the kids in that class, and they could hold conversations and grasp ideas, anything from "let's go get the good swings before anyone else does!" to "Hey did you see that movie last weekend on TV," all the way up to "Jesus I hate this school and that teacher." THAT didn't sound like a person with the same issues as the girl who rode our bus that had to wear a helmet to keep from injuring herself, and could not even speak recognizable words.

Why was Walter there?

As I liked to take my old, sweet time when it came to learning a thing or two when younger, a whole lot of memories and ideas came flooding back when I was married and a new father. What all those folks must have felt being treated that way just because they weren't happy in a small town, just because they did things differently, or had a traumatic event that really hit them hard, or even something they had no control over such as skin color, accent, or a limp, anxiety – just because they weren't "normal." To be shoved aside, or forced to behave, or labeled, boxed-in and forgotten if they weren't able to get away. Could be anybody.

The girl who lived nearby, my friend Walter, my mother. Me. My kids.

How suffocating. How sad. How infuriating.

I may be a lot of things because of my upbringing in that time and place, and I am truly revolted by my own words and actions on occasion – both remembered, and only assumed – toward those who I, personally, saw as different or *not normal*. I mean, I was a kid, and likely only modeling learned behaviors from the responsible adults around me, as well as good old fashioned peer pressure. But when everything gets shaken out in the wash, I like to think I have learned something since then, and *because* of those people I was around in my "formative years," both "good" and "bad." I am glad I was different enough, and surrounded by those who were just different enough, to appreciate the absolute weirdos and non-conformists that tend to gravitate toward me as I continue through life. It would be a LOT more boring and dull of a world without them.

OF PIGS AND METEORITES

My dad and I had a very complicated relationship for the vast majority of our adult lives. It was much simpler up until I was about 9 years old, but never easy. He never really trusted a word out of my mouth. And mind you, a LOT of words came out of my mouth when I was younger. So much so, that my father (I am hoping) affectionately nicknamed me "Motormouth." One day when we were working outside, my father, in what I have since learned is an expression of exasperation, forcefully shrugged his shoulders, turned to me, yanked his cigar out of his mouth, and growled – in a measured, exhausted tone just short of a cross-examination accusation

"Do you ever shut up?" He asked, staring straight down at me. "I will give you twenty dollars (a LOT of cash for a young boy who read 25 cent comic books in 1972) if you can keep your mouth shut for one hour."

I had since learned that my dad never asked a question that he didn't already know the answer to; and he was never wrong, and never apologized. He also never made a bet unless he knew he was going to win, or at least not have to pay out. But at this stage of my life, I was still all-in for any wager he cared to make with me. Perhaps I had a great deal of confidence. More likely, I just never knew when I was being played. In either case, I agreed. One hour, zipped lips, yeah boy.

"HA! I'll take that bet, father, hope you can back up that boastful wager with the paper, old man. Prepare to be parted with your hard-earned cash!" This was said in my head; what came out my mouth was actually something more closely resembling "Okay!"

The deal was sealed in whatever manner we sealed deals with at the time; he jammed his cigar back in his mouth, under the Snidely Whiplash facial hair he sported at the time, and turned around to get back to what house-related labor we were doing.

"Man," I thought to myself, "twenty bucks! I could not only catch up on all the back issues of Spiderman and Werewolf-by-Night comics at Hoffman's Pharmacy, but I could also grab quite a little sack of goodies from Walsh's book store – where there was a big candy counter as well as shelves covered with all manner of books. OOOH, yeah, Walsh's also had three of the new Conan the Barbarian book series available. Yeah, gonna get them too. Let me see… what else…" My mind raced as I helped haul away the trash that Dad was producing by tearing up what he was tearing up. "Maaannnnn, I'm going to still have money left over, even after all that stuff is…"

"Hey, what are we doing?" my brother Chris asked me as he walked up slipping on his work gloves.

"We gotta take all this stuff away and load it onto the wagon over there," I said without missing a beat. Look at that, not only was I earning money, but I was delegating. OOOOH! And also, I was now multi-tasking! That's grown-up level shit.

Chris went right to work. My dad stopped dead in his tracks, he did that shrug again. Why was he doing that, I wondered? I'm working. I have new skills. What's the problem now?

He turned back and looked at me, snorted a chuckle. "Wow, not even one minute."

My life and relationship with my father was pretty much just one long, extended version of this very exchange. Varying intensities, different levels of shouting, anger and disappointment – but pretty much *this*. Not believing anything I said, always expecting the worst, and a chronic, bemused "yeah, I thought so-itiveness."

I can't even say that it bothered me too much as a matter of course; I never really gave it much thought when I was younger, it only occurred to me when I was older. But there were specific times that stick in my mind, times when it mattered to me, times when it hurt a bit more than I cared to admit, times that were like bold-text punctuation to the rest of a paragraph that was one long run-on sentence. But now, they just make good stories.

We had a large pig pen at the top of the hill behind our barn, next to one of the 1800 square acres of garden we had to weed every day before the sun came up, kind of right at the tree line that separated the civilization of our well-groomed property with the wild backwoods.

We also had a little, maybe 100 square foot pen built in the barn where we would keep a piglet until it was big enough to hang out with the huge porkers up on the hill. Every day I had to feed the piglet, and then hump a 50-pound sack of feed up the hill to feed those guys.

One morning, as I got to the top of the hill, I heard loud squealing by the big pigs, and plenty of growling and non-normal livestockian activity coming from the Big Pen. I dropped the sack from my shoulder and ran over, stepping on the lower rail of the fence to boost myself up higher so I could see what was up.

Couple dogs, a husky and some mutt, had their teeth into one of our pig's hind legs and they were trying their hardest to get their breakfast To Go… it just wasn't real keen on going. The other pig was trying to de-motivate the dogs. I jumped off the fence rail and tore down the hill and ran inside the house to my father.

"DAD DAD THERE'S TWO DOGS UP IN THE PEN ATTACKING THE PIGS!" I blurted.

Dad, who loved a good opportunity to grab his nickel plated .357 revolver with magnum grips and maybe shoot something, grabbed his nickel-plated .357 revolver with magnum grips and ran out the house and up to the barn. Why was he running to the barn, my mind fleetingly asked; meh, he knows what he's doing.

As I caught up to him, he was standing just at the threshold of the barn opening, looking inside, obviously seeing the little piglet gamboling about in the straw, or whatever the hell it is that piglets do with their billable time. Clearly, no dog-led invasion that required gun-shooting or even a low-level bellowing. I mean, Jesus, I did say "...the PIGS," plural. Why did he even go to the barn? "Pigs" plural was up on the hill, "pig" singular was the barn. Should I have said "hogs" instead of "pigs?" I probably should have said "hogs."* Anyway... the plurality should have been enough; the mistake was clearly on him. I'm just saying.

It was The Look I got, as he turned his gaze, that got me. That "You filthy little lying shit, if there wasn't too much work involved with making you disappear into the woods I'd very likely do just that." THAT look. I balked a fraction of a second after being hit with that look, but quickly adjusted and blurted as I pointed in the general direction, "NO, the one up the hill!" blurted I.

Wow. He just started to turn back toward the house, quite probably trying to figure out which of the giant granite boulders on the property he could cram me under, when a squeal ripped through the air. "YES!" his face said, as it whipped back around toward the direction of the porcine scream, "THERE'S SHOOTING TO BE DONE!"

He split immediately, charging up the hill with me not too far behind. By the time I pulled up next to him close to the Big Pen – he was popping off shots toward the tree

---

* There is a difference between "pigs" and "hogs." Technically, a "pig" is a little hog, like under 120 lbs. While a "hog" is a big pig, over 120lbs. I think the pigs that were attacked were actually hogs. But I mean... come on.

line like Dirty Harry. I could vaguely see the dogs regretting the specific decisions they had recently made, as they hauled-ass through the trees east, toward freedom.

Dad's gaze did not leave that direction. "What kind of dogs?" he snarled.

"That big grey husky and the other one from…" I started

"The So-And-So's," he spat in a finish.

Never even looked at me, he just clomped back down the hill, hopped in his red State truck and sped down the road. "Fuck. I'd hate to have been the So-And-So's," I thought to myself. A few days later, the So-And-So's had two fewer dogs than they started the week with.

Dad never said a word to me about it again. No "thank you, no sorry I doubted you." Nothing. Meh, I was used to it. He wasn't going to say thank you, and he certainly wasn't going to admit any wrong doing on his own part, so it was pretty much just business as usual. Dad - 1, Greg - 0.

Now, strange and wonderful are the ways of the High Peaks, and I did get a tiny bit of vengeance later that summer. I would like to have thought it was closely juxtaposed to the Pig incident, but memory doing what it do, I honestly can't say with any certainty that it was. For the purpose of this story, we might as well say it was later that summer, because it sure felt like it was to me.

I was up late one night looking north out at the lake from my window on the second floor of our house; I have never been able to sleep, started as a kid I guess. Had a great view of the water, and in a full moon I could even see the waves. In the winter, the green glow of the Northern Lights shimmered brightly; and on any given, cloudless night, the stars put on a pretty good show as well.

On this summer night in question, about one or two in the am, I was looking out at the lake, and the western sky just FLARED up with red and orange – and this ball of flaming whatever – roughly the size of a softball held at arms length – shot in at a sharp angle and disappeared into the dark water.

"Did I just see a *meteorite* land in the lake?!" I thought. "I JUST SAW A METEORITE?!* Holy crap! I can't wait to tell…" Yeah that wasn't going to happen. Tell my dad I saw a meteorite land in the lake? No, no upside to that. I could maybe tell my brothers, but that would be a crap shoot and not worth the effort.

So the next day when we were out working in the yard, I said nothing about it to my father at first, but being the blabbermouth I was, something got said as I worked with him and my grandfather – and it triggered my mouth before my brain could catch up and quash it, and I blurted out what I had seen the night before.

Work stopped. Dad and Grandpa looked at me. Dad shook his head with a smirk, and started to work again; grandpa looked at Dad, then at me, then started to work again as well.

---

*Meteors apparently only exist while screaming through the atmosphere. Outside of the atmosphere – above (space) – they are meteoroids; they only become meteorites when they hit the Earth. Technically, I did not see it hit the Earth, just the water. So I guess I saw a meteor.

Well, that went as expected I thought.

And then, as if someone out in the sky had my back, our neighbor Margo walked up slipping on her work gloves, and the first thing out of her mouth – I am not lying – was:

"Did anybody else see that fireball drop into the lake last night – it was huge, about the size of a softball held at arms length?"

Mind you, Margo was nearly deaf, so there was no way she could have overheard the previous conversation.

Dad didn't even look at me, he looked at Margo as she started to work; my grandfather smiled without saying a thing. Dad said something dismissive, Margo did not back down, repeated almost exactly what I had said, it unfolded just like I saw. Something clearly splashed in the lake last night, and for all I know, Margo and I were the only two that saw it. I may have just been a kid, but she was a trained medical professional – and this was a completely unsolicited corroboration of the thingy that happened. Greg was on the board with a win.

Man, I started working with the strength of three kids my size, which really only amounted to like one grownup, but for me I felt like I could stack five cords of fire wood in 10 minutes. My inner voice kicked right in without even missing a beat:

"Yeah, where's my twenty bucks now, Dad?"

LOSING MY RELIGION

For not being religious in any way at all, I sure do like churches and gospel music. The architecture of the churches on the outside and inside, the decorating, the way sound sounds, that weird, sound booth sort of feel they have. And the music is just fun – Gospel music anyway, not necessarily the psalmy stuff.

I don't know why, I really don't, I haven't attended church for almost 50 years. The music I can get any time, any where with all the places to stream, and though I have no real reason to go to a church – I dig them when I'm near them or in them.

We had two churches on the road where I lived as a kid, and our house was just about smack-dab center between the two. As kids, we called them the Black Church and the White Church, but not for the reason you might think. It was simpler. One church what painted white, the other was black. Or rather a dark brown color. Whenever we went out to hang out with our friends, or to cause trouble, or whatever, we always said which way we'd be going by saying "down toward the white/black church."

As a Catlick family (as my grandparents might say) we attended St. John's – the black church. This quaint little church was actually my favorite of the two simply because of its architecture. I don't know if it was by design or if other factors played a part, but St. John's was not particularly flashy, as churches went. The exterior was finished out with rough-hewn waney-edge lap siding, and was actually painted or stained to that dark color, giving it a very dark, earthy tone and feel to it.

St. John's was even nice on the inside, very rustic, and felt very appropriately Jesusy and solemn. Simple in its construction, and even the religious icons were more on the subdued side – no overly-used flashy gold leaf nonsense.

The White Church, the Presbyterian Church, was pretty bland. Just your standard white shiplap siding, with a little steeple, much bigger parking lot, which is not to say it was a big lot, just bigger than St. John's. Both churches were fairly small, and were set on property that had the tree line right at the back. I imagine they sat about the same amount of folks, maybe 50-100 in the pews. I never actually set foot in the White Church, but it seemed about the same size on the outside.

We played in the parking lots quite a bit, of both churches, riding our bikes around, throwing a ball or Frisbee or whatever. But St. John's also had the only nearby tennis court; well, it had a net that stretched across, and could be raised or dropped using a hand crank.

The building itself was almost always left unlocked, so we could go in and get a drink of water at the fountain in the hallway when it was hot outside, or get in out of the rain if it surprised us while we were out. Or, if it so took our moods, we could also go inside and break into the supply cabinet and snack on the wafers for kicks, and stand up on the altar to see what it felt like to be a priest for a few minutes. No, we never got into the sacramental wine. At least I don't think so. I mean we had some class.

On Halloween, there was usually a party for the local kids, that had all the stuff you'd expect: the spooky music, the spooky foods and cookies, the spooky games with water that everyone had already stuck their filthy faces in to lick and bite floating fruit. It was fun.

Father Lattimer, who lived right next to the church, had one of those houses that had their bowl of candy out with an Honor System sign on it. I guess he figured we were all god-fearing members of the congregation, and we wouldn't *dare* take more than one piece. He would have been wrong, as all the kids took more than one. In fact, the only thing that separated the good kids from the bad kids on Halloween was the fact that the good kids may have taken 6 pieces, but the bad kids drained the bowl in one visit. So they were definitely going to a much worse Candy-Taker's Hell than we were.

Christmas and Easter were the two big holidays that were celebrated at church with masses, of course. Morning church for Easter, evening or midnight masses for Christmas. When we were old enough we'd walk to church, even when it was cold and snowing. It was kind of fun, really. On Christmas Eve there was always that special feel, and the music was loud and sounded very Noely. We kids got to open one present before heading to church, I guess to prime us for the next morning – or maybe to shut us up. On Easter we'd go home and have a big traditional Slavic breakfast, and then do our egg hunt – which was almost always inside, because it was still 105 below outside.

When our grandparents visited during either of these holidays, there was *always* a huge box of goodies brought from the city consisting of baked goods and some other foods our grandmother made, and then some gigantic "handmade" kielbasa and sausages from a deli. You know those Hillshire Farms Polish sausages or kielbasa you get in most grocery stores? Those are about half the size of the ones our grandparents got from their Slavic friends at the deli. We ate GOOD on holidays. If we didn't live on a farm and work so much, I fully expect that I would have weighed about 372 pounds by the time I was 12 just from the holiday food alone.

When I was in First Grade, for some reason, I was taken from public school and sent to attend the Catholic Elementary School in Saranac Lake with my brothers and sister. Saint Bernard's, or Saint Barnyard's or Saint Boneyard's as we kids called it. THAT was an experience, and I'm pretty sure, even after just one year of attendance, that all the stories everyone tells about the Nuns in a Catholic school are true. Sister Mary Yardstick, the knuckle-rapping – yeah, we had that. If it weren't for the goulash the cafeteria served on Wednesdays, I don't think there would have been a single thing that I enjoyed about being at that school.

We also had a pretty cool set of Monkey Bars sitting on the blacktop courtyard right outside my classroom. When I was little, that intertwined bar matrix seemed like it was twenty feet high, but it must have only been about 8 feet or so at most in reality. Still high enough to fall from and break something, which some kids did on occasion. Whatever the Catholic Nun version of "rub some dirt on it," was – that's what we got.

My brothers and sister and I were all pulled from St. Barnyard's after my First Grade year, which we all loved, and were stuffed back into public school. I never found out why that was – we still attended St. John's though. We attended for what seemed like ages, but I know for a fact that it was only until about 1973, so maybe seven years after we moved to the area. I know this because that was about the time our parents started to have marital issues, and from what I pieced together from a few different conversations with each of them separately.

We stopped going to church cold turkey immediately after our parents went to the priest for help/advice, and did not particularly care for the advice that was offered. They separated soon after, and we never went to church again.

As far as I know, no one in the immediate family ever went to any kind of church again, at least not with any regularity. I suppose that is sort of weird, you'd figure that at least one child or one parent would have continued it, just out of tradition or some such. All of us just stopped and never went back. And we never really talked about it either, well except for my mom. We had short chats about religion and the lack thereof quite a few times, for whatever reason the subject came up when we were older. But no steady Sunday trip.

My wife's parents were Catholic, and they also raised their kids Catholic, but really it was only her mother who attended church with any sort of regularity after we met.

We never saw eye to eye on religion, my wife and I; though I think in broad strokes we understand the arguments on both sides; and we went to services or mass very infrequently early on. But it just didn't ever coalesce for us. When our children were born, there was no major rush to baptize them. I saw no purpose to it at all, but it was important to my wife and her mother, and also to my paternal grandparents, so they got it. And even THAT was unconventional.

We baptized both children when our second was born – so one was a few months old, and one was almost five years old. Their godparents were a practicing Jewish person, and a self-proclaimed Communist; which of course we kept from all the pertinent parties present. There were no First Communions.

I think the hardest thing I ever had to do, religion-wise (or even just in general), was to tell my grandmother – when she was in the hospital for the last time – that I would do my First Communion, because we stopped the church-going before I had mine. My siblings were not so lucky – I have seen pictures of the little suits and dress. I know it meant a lot to my grandmother but it meant nothing to me.

Because it meant a lot to her, and she was dying, I told her I would do it. But also because I know it meant a lot to her, I wasn't going to go through the motions and be a complete blasphemous hypocrite, I just wanted her to be happy and at peace about the matter before she passed. Surely whatever force is out there would understand the intent and not tic off a mark next to my name that would follow me for the rest of my life. It made my grandmother happy, and I am pretty sure she would have understood.

A LESSON ON TRUST

My grandfather and I could get neck deep in some shit. And as it turned out, we could get ankle-deep in some shit if we dove blindly in head-first. This is my father's father, the nice guy, the even-keeled guy, the friendly guy with the same gap between his upper front two teeth that I have. The hard-working, just plod along until you did all you could do that day guy. He almost without fail always said at the end of a long work day where we accomplish a shit-ton: "Well, we didn't get much done today, Greg, but we'll knock the hell out of it tomorrow."

My grandfather could fix or make just about any-thing – he knew everything, or maybe he just figured it out as he went along, whatever the case, I have seen him fix electrical and plumbing issues, car issues, any house issue from framing to remodeling, and he built things out of wood as well. Bookcases, kids toys, even the baby crib for our two kids that he made alongside my dad.

I say all this because I had learned to trust whatever he told me to do, or whatever I saw him doing. He wasn't much of an "explain it to you" teacher, but he was one hell of a "watch him do it" kind of teacher. Whenever I worked with him, I knew at some point I would get what he was doing, and all the stuff leading up to it would make sense.

Mind you, he wasn't perfect, I get that. He sure didn't like confrontation; that's not to say he avoided it completely, but he was *very* particular about how and when he participated in it. Typically, when confronted with a verbal assault from friendly fire – say, either his son or his wife – he mostly just smiled and weathered the storm, only interjecting where explicitly required.

When the interaction was from strangers, he could be very shrewd and not-back-downable. In his late 70's he lived in an assisted living community. One night, out of boredom I suppose, he read the whole rules and regulations manual that came with the apartment. He noticed there was specific mention of a pool table and shuffleboard for use in the Day Room.

Only problem was, there were no such games in the Day Room. The other residents just said "Meh, they never bought them, and they brush us off when we ask about them. Don't even bother, it ain't gonna happen." A few weeks after my grandfather started asking about them, there was a brand new Pool Table and Shuffleboard in the Day Room. And the Administrative Staff gave Grandpa the side eye and a wide berth every time they saw him.

Yes, he was as stubborn as they get, and not always in a good way. He wouldn't go get hearing aids until he was into his 70s, and he had to be guilted into that.

My dad and I were heading back to the farm, when we saw Grandpa's car turn ahead of us from a cross-street – he was heading to the same place we were. We honked. No recognition from Grandpa's car.

We followed his car pretty close, and my dad honked at him the whole stinkin' way at different intervals, even at stop signs and lights: never a wave or anything. Grandpa just kept up at the speed limit, drove twenty minutes, and parked.

We pulled up right next to him 5 seconds later, and got out of the car. Grandpa – in actual surprise – raised his eyebrows and said "Hey Frank, where'd you guys come from?" Dad, being the gracious person he was, immediately said "Where'd we come from? I've been on your ass honking at you since we left Malone, you deaf old coot."

Grandpa just looked at me, then back at his son and shook his head. "The hell you were, get out of here." And went off to start his work day.

That wasn't even the catalyst that got him to get hearing aids, though. Like me, Grandpa may have taken his time when it came to understanding the morals from a spur-of-the-moment, snarky cautionary tale. What finally got him into a pair of ear-cheaters was this:

Later that summer, we were taking hay in, quite a few acres of it, big tractors, hay rakes, hay balers, etc., like you do. After it was baled tightly, we'd take a large flatbed trailer out and Grandpa would drive, I'd throw the big rectangular bales onto the flatbed, and Dad would stack them up. Grandpa would use his own judgement to figure out when it was time to pull forward, and almost every time it was a tad sooner than Dad thought he should – which he shouted to his father *every single time* – but Grandpa didn't hear it.

So on one occasion, Dad finished stacking quickly, whipped a wink my way, and shouted at grandpa to please hold up a few seconds, WAIT WAIT WAIT! Then he jumped off the flatbed right before grandpa could pop the clutch and yank forward to the next bales. Dad laid down on his back in the grass, arms and legs spread out wide like he was making hay angels or something, and Grandpa turned around to watch us lift and stack – then saw Dad laid out.

Grandpa slammed the tractor into park, then lurched up out of the driver's seat and walked over, just as Dad got up with his snark and laid into him.

"Yeah, I'll bet THAT got your attention," he boomed over the sound of the engine. "I was yelling WAIT WAIT WAIT, and you didn't even hear a word I said, did you? Get some Goddamn hearing aids!"

Grandpa just climbed back into the seat quietly to get back to work; but you better believe he turned to check every time from then on before pulling forward. And yes, he finally went and got hearing aids a short time later. I guess Dad remembered this 15 or 20 years later, when he went and got his own with no provocation from anyone. I often think of this incident as I approach the same age.

But to circle back around to the type of shit grandpa and I used to get into, here are a few examples to punctuate our relationship, and they also happen to be my own personal favorites.

In the early 80s, I drove up from Las Vegas to the farm in New York in my new (to me) car, a 1976 Mustang II, the one with the short block 302 in it. That car was FUN to drive. But because of the engine size and my lead foot on the highway, I was not particularly happy with the gas mileage it got. So I decided to take the AC out of the car, and while I was in there, I'd replace the motor mounts – because Ford didn't really beef up the frame when they dropped that 302 in.

As usual, Grandpa was there with me. His hands couldn't fit in the tight spaces so much anymore, and his wrists hurt all the time, but he was there offering support, experience, and fun to the job at hand. He said "Make sure to disconnect the battery before you start anything."

Then he handed me a long-handle box wrench to loosen the nut holding the ground cable to the post.

I slipped the box wrench over the nut and gave it a yank, it was pretty tight. Grandpa said to just "use some elbow grease," his term for putting your back into it. I did. The metal wrench easily turned, and I ended up pulling the wrench straight back into the positive cable post six or eight inches away on top of the battery, closing the connection between the posts.

When I came-to, I was on my back about six feet from the grill of my car, and Grandpa was standing over me, looking down, what passed for concern on his face.

"Do you know what you did?" he asked matter-of-factly.

"Yes," I croaked.*

"Okay. Don't do that again," he said, and turned back to the car.

Had either of us mentioned this incident, which occurred while Dad was out on patrol, that most definitely would have been the end of our working together on cars. Maybe. Likely.

But it is way worse when you get caught in flagrante delicto.

On another occasion, some years later, it was raining pretty steady, and we were not going to get anything done outside, so Dad had given us a stack of things to do inside. Grandpa and I worked our way through the stack, and slightly before lunch time we had this thing to do out in the workshop. Now as I said, I trusted my grandfather implicitly, and knew that whatever he was doing would eventually make sense, I would do whatever he told me to do without hesitation. And this was one of those times.

He walked around the shop grabbing this doo-dad here, these metal pieces there, had me hold the apparatus while he turned screws or bent metal, it was pretty quiet except for the sound of the work, and the rain pattering on the fiberglass roof.

---

* Connecting the two posts of a car battery with something metal, is like sticking a bobby pin in an electrical socket. Which I have also done. Why was I not supervised more often?

At one point the shit he was doing needed some more space so we took it out to the shop annex which was a no-floor overhang with one wall shared at the far end of the workshop. There was a longer bench out there and we laid out some tractor parts with the thing that grandpa was creating.

At one point, it clicked in my head, and grandpa saw this and said "Ah HAAA, your grandfather isn't crazy, is he," and smiled.

So I started to help him even more now, anticipating what he needed and so forth. It was more fun now that I knew what he was doing, and now I just wanted to see if it worked. He got the thing done, and we now needed to use the air compressor to finish what we are doing, I went inside, grabbed the portable compressor, brought it outside and set it on the damp boards just under the work bench, Grandpa said "go plug it in over there so we can see if this works."

I grabbed the power cord and stepped off the planks into 4 inches of muddy water and sloshed over to the socket, which was about four feet off the ground, and I had that damn plug about two inches from the socket...

And I stopped.

I looked at what my hands were doing, then I looked down at the four inches of water that I was standing in, then I looked back at my grandfather – who had his back to me and was giving his Frankenstein creation the final touches.

"What are you waiting for," he said, losing his patience just a tad, "plug it in already."

I looked back down at the plug, then back at Grandpa – who had now turned into Mr. Gower from It's A Wonderful Life – and I didn't know what to do. I mean, I *knew* what to do, but wasn't sure *how* to do it now, because I was in the middle of a huge brain fart.

Thankfully, whatever hesitation I had gave just enough time for the door to the shop to swing open, and Dad stuck his head out

"Hey, you two nitwits eaten ye…" And then he saw us, saw my hand, the socket, the water up to my ankles, Grandpa hunched over NOT looking at me.

"ARE YOU FUCKING KIDDING ME?" Dad bellowed, which made Grandpa look up.

"Hey Frank, what're you doing?" he asked.

Dad threw up his hands and turned away, snarling at the universe in general

"That's all I fuckin' need right now, to come home and find my fuckin..." he trailed off after he slammed the door and stomped away, his voice, while incoherent, pulsed in waves of varying volume. As sound waves move in all directions, I am certain the words have hit Mars by now, even counting that they dissipate the farther away they get from the source. At one point we heard the door slam on his truck; it peeled out, and angrily drove away.

Grandpa and I just stood there for a second or two listening to the rain.

At last he turned to me and said, just like a sassy kid "oooooh, he's aaaangry."

Then he noticed me near the outlet. "You might want to stand on those planks instead, what are trying to do electrocute yourself?"

The moral of the story – to me, in time – was: you can trust someone all you want, but there are times when common sense should just kick in. This damn sure was one of them.

The thing Grandpa was making worked, by the way. We finished our chores, and thankfully, we didn't embarrass Dad in the community by being dead when he got home later that evening.

Grandpa fist-bump.

YOU THINK YOU HAD IT BAD?

We have two children; they're okay. My wife and I joke about being able to "return them," but we "don't have the receipt." It *really* is just kidding around. Because we *really* cannot find the receipts.

Despite what our kids think, they had a pretty easy upbringing, indentured servitude wise. I mean, compared to what *some* kids had to do, our children's particular lack of menial labor may have been a direct inverse result of the childhoods their parents had, so we tried to overcorrect. Tale as old as time.

We would have simple chores for them: take out the trash, wash the dishes, clean their rooms, that sort of stuff. Correct me if I'm wrong, but that stuff felt like nothing very difficult. And yet, even with *all that work* to do, they *still* found time to complain about the quality of their lives and threaten to call CPS on us as parents.

"You guys have got it EASY," I'd reason, "why, when I was a kid…"

Before I could finish my sentence, there would be between one and four wet thuds heard from the floor, where any number of eyes had been rolled back so far into heads that they found that little secret groove behind the ears where a rolled eye can slide out through the auditory canal and drop to the floor. They would reach for their respective eyes, which I would then nudge farther away with the toe of my left foot. As they patted around the floor in vain, I would tell them JUST what I had to do as a child.*

My day started at Still Dark O'clock, when I'd have to get up and get the chickens fed and watered. The chickens, layers and eaters, lived at the top of the hill behind the barn, so at one or two points in the week, there would be a lugging of a sack of feed up said hill, and emptying it into a metal trash can that could be sealed tight with a metal lid. The can was stored inside the little secondary pump house right at the very top of the hill.

Then I'd have to get them water, collect eggs from the layers, collect dead chickens if there were any, stuff them in a plastic bag and tie it tight and dispose of them. Then feed the turkeys, same deal with the dead ones. The

---

* I know I had siblings, and they likely helped in some way with these chores; but it never *really* felt like they pulled their weight. For all practical appearances – I was on my own.

times I *really* enjoyed this work, oddly enough, was in the winter months, because there were times in the winter when getting up at the dawn of time meant there might still be a bright moon up, or even stars or Aurora Borealis up there, shining down on the snow bright as day. It was quite a sight.

In the spring, our favorite pastime was shoveling the winter's-worth of shit out of the chicken coop. This was done by chopping the 4-inch-thick, 100-sf mat of compressed poop up like some sort of really unappetizing lasagna, and shoveling square sections of it into wheelbarrows. To this day whenever I smell ammonia, I am instantly transported back to that springtime poopcoop.

The pigs got their slop, which was literally slop in the very sense of the word. A wet mushy glop made from grain and water and any leftover food from the house that was trashed. I'd mix that up in some 5-gallon buckets and stand on the bottom rail so I could reach over the top rail and dump that into the trough just on the other side of the fence.

The pigs were cool, I always liked them. Kind of cute when little, and still sort of cute up to certain size and age. They'd hear me clonking about on the fence, and their ears would prick up, and I'd hear the first few exploratory grunts from the shed. But as soon as that slop started to slosh into the trough, it was grunt-n-trot city, as they charged the steaming Flavor Boat.

The trough was actually wide enough for at least four good-sized hogs to eat from at once, but for some reason, all three hogs always wanted to eat from exactly the same spot. A lot of head nuzzling and shoving ensued, as they gobbled down the tasty noms, occasionally looking up and happily snorting goo from their mouths and noses.

Of all the animals we raised, I liked the pigs the best (Don't tell the chickens, turkeys, rabbits or sheep that). To tell the truth, I was glad we didn't process those guys ourselves, it would have been more difficult. They are smart critters, playful too. If it weren't for the prospect of starving to death if we didn't consume them, I maybe would not have eaten them.

Indeed even today, I do not tend to eat a lot of pork simply because I know how smart they are, and I still sort of love the faces. Conversely, I also know that an even half-grown hog could make a meal out of me in seconds if motivated to do so. So that's what I tell myself when I have a pulled-pork sandwich at any number of BBQ joints near Austin.

Turkeys and sheep, on the other hand, we are doing them a favor turning them into meals, they just don't know it because of how dumb they are. The weird thing is I never really cared for lamb much, even though it should be mandatory to eat them by the handfuls right out of the box. Rabbits, of course, play the cute card every time. The ears, the noses, the jelly bean toes – it was difficult making a meal out of them if you stopped to appreciate the Cute Factor.

After these animals were dealt with, there was a dog and sometimes a cat to feed, then myself to feed, then a bus to catch to school. Some mornings, I was running a tad late, and I would get to school and notice I still had chicken shit all over my boots as I stuffed them into my locker and changed into my sneakers. Some days I even forgot to bring my sneakers, soooo... yeah, the smell followed me class to class.

After school I'd get home, usually to an empty house, well at least empty of responsible adults – until my grandparents moved in. My brothers usually had sports or something after school – how convenient. When I was alone, I had the same ritual every day: grab a sleeve of Ritz crackers and the peanut butter and jelly, and sit at the table watching M*A*S*H and Match Game 75 – or whatever year it was – while I did my homework.

Then it was quick check on the animals again, and then light weeding of gardens and picking anything that was ready to go. On the weekends was the heavy, in-depth weeding of what seemed like twelve acres of corn across the street, and then the same amount of other veggies way up on the hill on the other side of the pig pen right at the tree line, where any large animal could have snatched me as I worked. Large Animals abounded back then. I knew they were in there, watching, waiting for their chance. So I weeded *fast*. Maybe I missed some weeds. But I am alive today, so *who* was overreacting?

After the boiler plate chores on weekends there was whatever other big project was at hand – tearing something down, building something new, painting a building, shoveling shit, fixing a tractor, clearing over-grown trails, digging a pit, filling in a pit – any numbers of things. Sometimes the work our dad gave us felt very Cool Hand Luke-ish.

In the fall, this is where life got BUSY. All the gardens had to be harvested, processed, canned, frozen, pickled and put away. Entire sets of days were spent on beans, crabapples, and corn alone. Some years we had enough apples from these ancient orchards up on the hill to press our own cider, the waste from that went to the pigs and chickens, which they LOVED.

The smells in the house were incredible when we got to making jellies and jams. We had this huge crabapple tree right off the back porch, deer would come down in the fall to eat the apples that fell. One time a black bear was spotted eyeing the tree. It would take what seemed like days to completely pick that tree dry; and to reach the top branches, our dad devised an incredibly safe, OSHA-approved system. He put some planks on top of the equipment rack on his state truck, which he would park at different places under the tree.

Then he would put a 6-foot step ladder on top of the planks, and then he, himself, would get us kids to climb the ladder and pick the crabapples. The lightest one of us was the best and obvious choice for the ladder, cause you wouldn't want it to get top heavy. And if that lighter child were to fall to his certain death, well, we just wouldn't need that many jars of crabapple jelly that year.

Then came the fire wood. Our dad, being state employee, meant there was literally no end to the amount of raw materials he was able to choose from to get our fill. The rangers were always clearing trails somewhere, and the trees they had to dismantle were stacked neatly, seasoned a year or so, and then the wood was free to any takers. We were the takers. And we *took*.

Some years it really felt like he had nearly 300 acres worth of trees dumped in our parking area next to the house. Weeks were spent cutting the big logs into small logs, the splitting the small logs into firewood-shaped pieces, and then loading wheel barrows, schlepping those over to the new storing quarters ad nauseam, and then doing all over again day after day after day.

We'd fill up the side porch, the basement, the side of the house – any spare space that was within a very short walk of the various fireplaces we had in the house, would get stacked to the gills with fire wood. The cellar was actually sort of fun to fill, because one or two of us would chuck all the firewood down into the old coal chute off the back of the house, then the others would crawl up the chute from the cellar and move it farther down, and then arm-load it to the other side of the cellar. It felt very Charles Bronson-y in The Great Escape.

Once again, when winter set in, we were glad to have all that wood at the ready, but in the Fall, it was the bane of our existence. Do you have any idea how much fire wood can be generated by three grown-assed people who have just rented a log splitter, and also have a fairly unlimited supply of Molson? A LOT.

The pile of split firewood that we had to move and store was literally about 8-9 feet high and had a radius of about 15 or 20 feet. It was BIG. We'd use our wagon on the tractor, wheel barrows, and even loading up our arms to move it where it needed to go. Mind you, when a log is split, it makes pieces that look like really long, fat axe heads. Like a slice of pie shaped but extended out like a cylinder, so that the point of that pie slice became a jagged sharp edge over a foot long.

We'd pile these fat axe heads up into our arms and walk them 200 feet to where they needed to live for a few months – even with long sleeves, we ended each day with chop marks and slashes and splinters in the crooks of our arms. We could have died from exhaustion more than once, but Dad would NOT tolerate quitters. It was WORK.

In the winter, we had pretty much the same type of chores, but we now had eight feet of snow and 20-below temperatures to do them in. And I am not even exaggerating on the weather. We may not have had to walk 13 miles uphill in the snow to school every day, but we had the snow and the temperatures to do it in. Google the temperatures in Saranac Lake some time – some of the lowest in the country in the winter.

In that weather, we now had to still take care of the animals that were not turned into happy meals, plus whatever specialty projects still needed doing, plus snow shoveling, and ice chopping and fire wood to bring inside for the many wood burning stoves we had, and so forth.

In the spring, we had yet another huge undertaking added to the heap, but at least this one was a bit more fun. We made Maple Syrup.

Somewhere out in the woods between Upper and Middle Saranac Lakes, a family friend owned some rather historic land that he and his wife were renovating. On one patch of this land there was a sugar house surrounded by acres and acres of Maple trees as far as the eye could see. This friend let us use the house every spring to tap and drain trees, boil the crap out of the sweetest sap ever until it was thick and amber-colored. Then we'd bottle up (actually, they were 1-gallon rectangular tin cans mostly, and little glass bottles) about five thousand gallons of the stuff and sell that out at our roadside stand as Pure New York State Maple Syrup.

I 100% blame my life-long syrup-snobbery on this.

However, even this fun activity required a lot of work, – surprise surprise – chopping and stacking firewood for the enormous, long sugaring stove, washing the huge rectangular pans and plugs, shoveling snow, hustling empty buckets and covers and taps and hooks to the trees, and sloshing full buckets to the bulldozer-dragged tank-sled for emptying – it just never ended.

And then as adults, we now had to put up with our own children, whining about having to wash their own damn spoons after they polished off the ice cream right out of the container – which they left under the bed for three weeks until it got ants. And we ain't allowed to beat them? And we can't return them without a receipt? The struggle is real.

Life just is not fair.

ALL FUN AND GAMES

Sometimes you just wanted to get away. As nice as the area was where I grew up, a steady diet of *only* that can feel confining, or maybe get a bit stale. Fear not, however, because there were so many other little villages and towns and smaller cities to visit within a decent drive. And many of these small communities had some rather fun attractions for kids and adults alike.

Land of Make Believe was a really fun, story-book-themed park in Upper Jay; Wilmington had The North Pole with Santa's Workshop; Schroon Lake had Frontier Town; and Upper Canada Village was a bit of a drive over near Massena, but on the Canadian side of the river. So there were lots of places to go have fun for the day.

For those willing to drive a bit more, there was a huge assortment of other attractions and destinations.

Lake George is a quaint little village downstate from us, about halfway between where we lived and the Capital of Albany. And it had one of our favorite amusements parks ever when we were kids: Gaslight Village.

This park was set up like a Victorian turn-of-the century-town with – you guessed it – gas lamps lining the streets. There were rides, games, a theater for bigger shows/concerts and something for everyone. "Yesterday's Fun Today" was the slogan, and the park actually was well-liked by both kids and adults. We loved going there, I personally would have lived there if possible. Bodee-oh-doooh, doh DOH!

When we were all still a family, Mom and Dad and us four kids, we'd take these day trips on the weekends, and of course longer trips during the summer. There was even a long road trip we took one summer to Virginia, where a friend of Dad's from his Navy days had invited us to visit. The farm his friend lived on was pretty sweet, especially for kids. There were petrified fossils on the property, courtesy of the ancient sea bed that used to occupy that entire area, and it was so easy to scrape the surface of the nearby cliff to find them in abundance.

We helped with chores during the time we spent there, feeding the animals, cleaning stalls and whatnot. But our favorite activity was one that was taught to us by our new friends. In the second-story hay loft of the barn, there was a trap door that was used to drop hay down for the sheep below. Above the trap door was a thick rope that could be dropped down to the pen below. Children, if properly disengaged from all thoughts of common logic and safety, could climb down the rope, make faces at the huge angry ram, and then try to clamber back up the rope before the charging animal connected massive curled horns with supple skin, snappy bones, and released a few pints of blood in a colorful, misting spray.

During that trip, we stayed at campgrounds, sleeping in our gigantic WWI surplus canvas cabin tent that comfortably slept an entire regiment of adult soldiers. The khaki-colored tent had wooden poles that held up the spine and corners, and heavy steel stakes that attached the whole shebang to the ground.

When neatly packed into the convenient carrying case, the entire Buick-sized package weighed about 1400 pounds. Our dad would haul this off the roof of the Country Squire, or load it back up there all by himself. Anytime we kids had to move that tent, it damn near took all four of us. I am certain to this day that the only reason Dad used this tent, was to make sure we kids knew how strong he was, as a preemptive measure.

This summer trip was very memorable to me, and I assume, to all my siblings as well. We spent a lot of time in the family station wagon, made a lot a side-trips to historical sites along the way, and learned a lot of new limits to Mom and Dad's patience. I don't think we ever had as big a vacation as that one again as a family, and certainly not as far away from home.

As memorable trips go, one very specific trip that sticks in my mind was the summer my mom and I went by ourselves on a day trip to Lake George. I don't recall there being a reason we went, and it wasn't planned very far in advance, I guess she just needed a day away; which was more than fine with me, because I didn't have to share anything with my siblings – food, fun or time – I just did what I wanted to do, and of course what my mom wanted to do.

In addition to the Vaudeville-themed Fun Park – there was a new attraction called House of Frankenstein's Wax Museum that had recently opened (so I am guessing this was circa 1973). I was HUGE into Monsters at that age, loved the Hammer films of Frankenstein, Dracula, The Mummy, etc. – couldn't get enough of them; so when I heard about this new place, I was thrilled.

House of Frankenstein was like a more robust Halloween haunted house that was open all year round, with a nifty gift shop to stock up on those white slip-on fangs and fake blood and bloodshot plastic monster eyes. I spent so much money in that gift shop.

We went to House of Frankenstein, had a really good time, it was pretty high-end – or at least it felt that way to me. So bloody, so macabre, so canned-screamy and chain-rattley. THIS, I thought, channeling phrases that were not invented yet, was my jam.

Then we went to Gaslight Village afterward and rode the rides, ate the junk food and played the games.

We saw Mario Manzini, a sort of Elvis-meets-Houdini type of escape artist, who actually performed the trick that made ol' Harry famous – the Milk Can Escape. It was pretty impressive to see him stuffing himself down into that metal milk can as the water displaced out the sides. We had a few of those old milk cans in our barn, the thought of being jammed into one gave me a case of the Jeebies.

We even managed to meet Mario and visit with him backstage for a bit afterward, and I got to see a bunch of his tools of the trade up close, I was even able to take a look at the milk can and verify that it was, indeed solid metal, no escape hatches. Then I got manacled for a few minutes while I tried to figure out how to take them off.

Later in the evening we saw Tony Orlando and Dawn perform on the big stage. Well, my mom saw most of it, I was too short to see much, until a total stranger next to us asked if he could lift me up on his shoulders so I could see some of the show – Tony Orlando was HUGE back then. I saw them dancing and singing on the stage, it was the very first first-hand sighting of celebrities for me. So that was extra special.

Later that night, as the Village was closing down, we went to get one last bite to eat before we hit the road for the two-hour trip back home. We stopped to get a huge slice of pizza, which was lovingly squeegeed of oil, slapped on a paper plate and plopped on the counter in front of us by some surly pizza-stand employee who looked like he just *loved* his job *so much*.

The server stated the cost, and mom dug through her purse to find the money. She started with paper, went quickly to coins, and soon ended with her being one penny short. Mom looked at me, looked up at the pizza guy – who was a total dick, by the way, for not giving the pizza to us and eating the penny shortfall. She was getting a tad frazzled – it was a long day.

She turned around for a second or two, staring off into space, huffing out a breath. Then she looked down at the ground – and there at her feet... was a penny.

She picked it up, slammed it on the counter and gave the guy such a look, may he rot in Hell. We took the pizza slice and ate it on one of the old timey iron benches under the light of a gas-powered street lamp, and then we started the drive home.

It was a fun day, and I may have forgotten all of the exact details, but I never forgot the day, and the time with Mom having fun in Lake George.

Even as a kid though, there was a weird feel to that trip, couldn't quite put my finger on it exactly. I admit that at the time, I never really thought about it much though, being the somewhat self-absorbed child that I was. But there was *some little itch* up in my brain case that I couldn't quite scratch.

It was only years later that I put two and two together and figured out the other layer of what was going on with that day away. It was during the summer after third grade, and by fourth grade my mom no longer lived in the house with us anymore. Ahhhh... *there* it was, scratch scratch.

I looked at those same events with a different filter after that, seeing the shows, riding the rides, playing the games – my mom didn't participate in a lot of them, she sat and watched me play and ride. Not finding that last piece of change she needed in her purse, she had literally spent every penny she had to make sure I had fun. And that penny on the ground? That was – as she would say often in the ensuing years – the "Universe looking out for her."

I never "believed" in "the Universe" much, or perhaps just not that version. I'll tell you what, though, I'm glad that someone dropped a penny and couldn't be bothered to pick it up so that my mom could have a great day away with me without the very last thing that happened was she couldn't buy us a slice of pizza to eat.

Nice move, Universe. Well played.

Just sHy of Heaven

The little patch of land we lived on when I was 2-ish until I was 14-ish, was a *really* nice little patch of land. If you have never been to the Adirondacks – especially the northern part where they got the High Peaks – you are really missing something. Go. Visit. If for no other reason, than just for the AMAZING prize you get once you've joined the 46ers.

But please do not actually visit, because tourists always mess things up for the locals. Well, honestly, the locals can go suck a Brook Trout; tourists always mess things up for the nature. You know, just take my word for it – THE MOST fabulous natural setting on the entire globe.

Anywhich, the landscape was truly overwhelming. The trees, the lakes, the huge granite mountains, lovingly carved everywhere you want to be by kinder, gentler gla-ciers a way long time ago. Animals out the whazoo; you couldn't swing a dead chipmunk around your head with both hands without hitting a loon, and by the way up in that part of heaven, we called that a Thursday night.

The only blemish on the area, and I do mean the ONLY blemish – which by the way was not really noticed by the kids who loved it – was the fact that somebody went a tad apeshit with the allocation of winter months, vis-a-vis snow and ice and cold temperatures.

I live in Texas currently, where my wife complains that there are no such thing as seasons. The longer we stay here, the more I am inclined to agree with her. It's just always hot, but for a few weeks during "FallWinter-Spring" it gets less hot. Occasionally, someone in charge screws up and we get snow. A few years ago, we got snow for an entire week, like eight inches. And it was nine below. How are we supposed to live like that? That's inhumane.

I know, I know, I joke because it's true. There really aren't much in the way of seasons, but because of this, a week of really bad weather once in 100 years ain't so ter-ribly bad, although it could really do a number on you.

What is terribly bad is the weather up in the High Peaks region; or at least it was when I was a kid. The en-tire planet has seemed to take a turn for the warmer in the ensuing 40 years, almost like a planetary hottening has been occurring. But back in the day?

Springs, Summers, Falls – there was not a bad day in the lot. An endless buffet of greenery, and bluery, sunnery and rainery; tra-la-la skipping through the marshes and standing on the mountain tops with outstretched arms, as rainbow trout jumped up out of the water, slathering themselves with butter, salt-n-pepper before snuggling into your sizzling frying pan, content in the knowledge that they would be eaten as fresh as fresh gets.

That first bite of buttery trout would be half-way to your mouth on a 900-dollar German-engineered REI foldable camping fork, and BAM! Twelve feet of snow piled on top of you, and refused to leave for 16 months straight.

We used to go to school in the bus behind a snow plow some mornings, six-foot drifts piling up as we went. You know how bad it had to be to get a "Snow Day?" Well let's just say that the vocabulary of the North Country does not contain words for the idea of a "Snow Day." The entire plumbing system for the school would have had to rupture and coat the building in three inches of solid ice before we could even *conceive* of hearing that school was cancelled for a day. And even on those days, hockey practice just started earlier and ended later. We had SNOW.

The snow and cold stayed a long time, as I said before, but it did not last forever. There was always a period of time when the sun came out, the snow went away and we were able to hike, and fish, and canoe, and camp, and grow gardens, and run in the fields. And when *that* day was over, we'd have snow again.

I swear before the St. Regis fire tower and The Seven Carries, the latest in the year I ever saw "snow" was at the beginning of June. I recall raking and doing some lawn care activities with my dad, grandfather and neighbor one day. My dad got a weird look on his face and looked up, shrugged and went back to work. Then my grandfather and neighbor did the same thing, causing my father to look back up again.

"I'll be dipped," he said.

I looked up. Not a great deal of them, but holy crap, there were snowflakes coming down in June.

As bad as the winters were back then, and may still be today, at least they did have their upsides. The skiing and snowmobiling aside, one of the best perks to the freezing winters was this: the unabashed slaughter of entire legions of black flies.

Black flies, you ask? What's so bad about black flies? Why, they don't even have an interesting name, I mean aren't most flies blackish in color? And they are just flies. Shoo them away, perhaps introduce them to the business end of your old pal the Fly Swatter. I mean surely something so innocuous could not tarnish the good name of the idyllic fields, streams, and peaks of the of this land just shy of heaven?

You fools.

There are houseflies, which flit around your house as if they are a lure at the end of the line on God's fly-fishing rig, apparently with a little Fly Kink for your right hand's third knuckle. There are horse flies, which are basically houseflies with a flamboyant dress code and a penchant for coke and showing you what assholes they are with the teeth and the biting. There are Deer Flies, which have chunks of horse flies in their morning stool and apparently have the notion that your upper arm is an asteroid that is heading toward Deer Fly Earth, and they have to land, drill an oil rig derrick deep into your arm, place an explosive and then blow your flesh apart so the now smaller pieces of your arm no longer pose a threat.

And then there are Black Flies.

Black Flies, about the size of a gnat, a third the size of a grain of rice. In American Standards and Measures terminology, roughly 1/800,000th of a football field covered in elephants. BUT – they have, instead of mouth parts, tiny little pick-axes that they start slogging into your flesh immediately upon contact. Their flight plans follow a path that very disrespectfully was designed to ONLY pass through your eyes, ears, nose and mouth holes, and – and this is the kicker – they only travel in groups of 4 trillion or so.

The Mayor of Cold River, the Honorable John Rondeau, once wrote a poem, an ode if you will, to Black Flies (point of order: there is no singular form of the name, they are always referred to as "Black Flies" the plural, and some if not all local colloquialisms usually include some form of spitting swear word in front of it). An abridged form of the poem is herewith submitted, transcribed from the original Hermitaen Script:

> *Flitflitflitflitflitbitebiteflitearsnosemouth*
> *Bitebitebiteflitflitflitflitbitenose*
> *Mouthoohyouleftyouranusuncovered*
> *Forthreesecondsflitflitflitbitebiteflitnoseagain*
> *mouthagain*
> *Flitflitbite*

Black Flies were recently – well in the latter half of the 19th century – recognized by the Pope over in Vatican City, as absolute proof of the existence of the Devil and all the evil in the world. In fact there is a famous quote by Pope Benedict XIX, upon being presented with a cloud of Black Flies as a gift from a famous French explorer: "quid ipse infernus, Deus?!"*

I know they sound a bit daunting, and one might consider canceling a much-anticipated visit to the High Peaks after learning of their existence; but fear not, for there is a way to keep oneself from being tormented from this blight on existence. In 1971, at the famous Trudeau institute in Saranac Lake, a study was started to see what might be done about Black Flies in an attempt to make life easier for residents and visitors alike.

Three groups of test subjects were gathered, one of native residents of the area, one of visitors from states where Black Flies have never been reported, and a third control group of unidentified mixed subjects.

The study ran for three years, into October of 1974, during which time the test subjects were repeatedly exposed to varying volumes of Black Flies. Subjects were anything from completely naked, to covered head-to-toe with varying layers of clothing.

Soaps, perfumes, foods, nonconsumables such as motor oils, paints, organic matter and the like were all intro-

---

* "What the actual HELL, God?!"

duced in carefully applied doses, and particular attention was placed on time of day, time of year, and proximity to bodies of water from mountain lakes to marshy bogs.

So eager were scientists to figure out a "cure" to the Black Flies issue, that all the data was processed almost immediately as it was gathered, and in the Museum at Blue Mountain Lake there are still a few of the original ledger books and hand-written notes by none other than Dr. Francis Trudeau, Jr. himself.

Even a layperson was able to understand the scope of the study, as the scientists working on it day and night wanted there to be complete transparency to the public so that once the "cure" was discovered, there would be as many of the population as possible on-board to help employ it, and to finally be done with this blight.

On December 14th, at a news conference in the Harrietstown Town Hall on the corner Main Street and the George LaPan Highway in Saranac lake, the results of the study were disseminated to an eager crowd of press, notable business leaders and general population alike. The study, understated, yet aptly named "Black Flies: What Can Be Done," came up with a simple summary.

> *"In order to have a quality of life in the*
> *Adirondacks that was not greatly diminished*
> *by the presence of Black Flies... it helps*
> *greatly if one were not such a little bitch."*

It should be noted, that the obnoxious ending to this complete waste of time, fake scientific study story conducted to beat Black Flies, is a metaphorical embodiment of how Black Flies actually make you feel, but without the welts.

Without Black Flies, the Adirondacks would be the very portrait of a life most beautiful, Elysian Fieldish, even. But as it stands, they are here for the long haul. Any foray out to the backwoods, or even the front woods, or down to the lake or crossing the street to get the mail would have to be preceded by a ten-minute dance of slathering bug repellent all over any exposed skin.

Cutter made this little bottle of off-white cream that did a fair-to-midlin' job of keeping a lot of bugs at bay, including mosquitos, gnats, and no-see-'ems. The great thing about Cutter's bug cream was that it was thick and oily, which took the Black Flies a second or two to eat through before they could pick-axe your flesh.

But those in the know, they used Def-Con-rated Ole Woodsman Fly Dope. Ole Woodsman was THE SHIT, and literally looked and smelled like it too. Made from the same recipe as when it was introduced in the late 1800's, it did a fantastic job of rendering almost any living thing into a puff of plasma smoke: mosquitos, horse flies, deer flies, ticks, raccoons, osprey, Big Foots, and other humans.

The only bad thing about it was that because of the Uranium 235 content, you could not put Ole Woodsman product directly into your eyes, ears, nose or mouth, which was precisely where it was needed most for Black Flies. Come on, Ole Woodsman, you're better than that... try harder, or at least have a waiver for us to sign so we can slather our mucous-lined orifices at no fault to you.

The clouds of these tiny flying critters is truly exasperating; shaking your head side to side very quickly every quarter-second every second, to dislodge the little assholes is enough to have you rethinking your list of "Pros" that brought you to the North Country to begin with.

Those of us who grew up there knew the secret: just put up with the black flies until the sweet frozen ice and chill of winter dropped and made everything better. After 14 months, you would forget... until that one day of summer when it started all over again.

Soooo, other than *that,* there is absolutely nothing wrong with the Adirondacks.

Just keep in mind... the North Country is not for wimps; it never was.

VIRGINIA IS FOR ANXIETY

Shit scares me. Always has. But especially when I was younger. I really don't know why, I have just always had a lot of anxiety – mostly about the unknown or untried. My sweet spot was the Comfortable Rut, because I knew how things worked in The Rut; so if nothing ever changed, I'd be set for life.

But things did change. So staying in my Comfy Rut was not a sustainable option. But I also still didn't want to try anything new. I can't even tell you how many times I just backed out of things I was signed up for, was maybe even excited about at one point – just because I was anxious about actually getting there and doing the thing, and not knowing what I was doing.

What a stupid fucking thing to worry about: absolutely ly everything new.

I have since (sort of) learned how to deal with this dumb anxiety to some extent, but it took me *years* just to get to this level of Functional Angst. I think, like with a lot of other things, what helped me lose the idiotic anxiety was having kids. Every single thing you do after having a child is brand new and you have zero experience doing it, so I was constantly bombarded with angst, but I could not let it get the best of me.

And then when my kids started to show signs of the same irrational fears, I wanted to be able to help them, or at least explain it until they were bored with it. You know, like when your kids ask you where babies come from, and you just start boring them with the tedious facts, they just roll their eyes and walk away, now armed with pertinent info about it, but not wanting to dwell on the matter, and so they don't think about it at all, because now they know? You know? I don't know.

I think back on specific times I just plain dicked myself out of having fun because of the fear of not already being very good at something. Like going to school dances, or learning how to skate better so I could play hockey, or thinking about my future, of going to college or whatever. What a waste of brain cells. What a waste of time.

When I was in Cub Scouts, we once had an opportunity to go see how a McDonalds worked, and tour the one location we had over near Lake Placid. I wanted to know how it worked, I wanted to see the store, where all the magic happened that turned out the wonderful food that we got only every once in a while.

But when the day came, I called out sick. Why did I do that? I mean, I wouldn't have even been required to deep fry apple pies, or plate a cheeseburger, or fill a cup with a shake so thick the vacuum created by trying to suck it through the straw would actually implode and suck a lung back into the cup. So why then was I so afraid of going?

I loved winter and winter activities and sports, and always loved sledding on the hills by our house. Yet, one time the Scouts managed to get us a day on Mount Van-Hoevenberg – where the Olympic bobsled run was – *and* we were going to be able to take the run in an actual official bobsled. Guess what I did? Yes. That. The absolute Hell was the matter with me?

So by the time I was in my first year of high school, I was a mess, or at least I felt I was a mess. I was pretty tired of never going and doing things that I knew I would likely enjoy, and it made me uptight as all get-out. Then, as fate would have it, I learned of the next biggest change that my young life was going to have to deal with: my mom was going to be leaving the state.

The moves downstate were easy for me, I may have been apprehensive about the bus rides at first, but I got over it. I was able to deal with the move in-town, the move to Glens Falls, the move to Albany; but now she was going away to a completely different world that was on the other side of the planet where people looked completely different, they ate weird things, spoke another language and didn't take kindly to strangers – especially up-tight young fraidy-cats like me.

She was moving to Virginia.

Her new husband had joined the Air Force, and he was getting stationed at Langley AFB down in the Chesapeake Bay area. She might as well have been going to Abu Dahbi. What did I know about Virginia? I mean, other than I was born there.

Gaaaaaahhhhh!

What to do, what to do? Luckily, the relationship with my father had deteriorated, and living in his house was getting to be more than I wanted to handle, so that helped light a fire under my ass to make a decision on which I wanted to do less – stay at home, or try something new.

I did so much research; and this was in the days before the internet. I looked at maps, I tried to find pictures, I read information in the encyclopedias at school and at the public library. I was building up so much anxiety thinking about what people would look like and act like, and where I would find food, and what if, Heaven forbid, I got lost and wandered into the DMZ between the Hill People and the Lake People?

That was a LOT of pressure on a young person. To make matters worse, I then had to have that conversation with my dad, that I wanted to go live with my mother now. It went surprisingly well, as he chose the surprising route (sarcasm) of just not speaking to me much after I brought it up.

The drive down to Albany to drop me off with my meager belongings was a long and quiet drive, and at the time it did not occur to me that unlike my bus trips, I would not be returning to the North Country again. I remember passing the things I knew on the oft-driven way out of the BFE – familiar names and things whipped by: Ray Brook, Whiteface Mountain, Keene, Elizabethtown, that place just off the Northway where a pipe stuck out from under a rock in the mountain where you could fill a jug with *the absolute best-tasting* water you ever had. It all sort of blurred together and faded as I left the area.

I saw the sign for Ticonderoga, and boom, I was gone from the only home I had ever known, and it was like I was never there.

I think I was just too focused on trying to figure out how I would survive not only Virginia, but now the added pressure of living in Albany for a few months first. By the time Saratoga Springs and Schenectady popped up, it all became real.

My sister was already living down there, and so there was sort of a built-in support system of sorts – her friends. We got along okay, I went out with them often enough, but they were city folk, and their level of hanging out was *greatly* different from mine. I liked climbing trees and running through the woods; they liked chillin' in the tricked-out basement and being cool.

We'd sit in the basement of my sister's boyfriend's house listening to the new albums from Michael Jackson, or Peaches & Herb, and her friends tried to teach me to dance new steps like the Bump or the Hustle, which were *really* hard to do with a board up my ass. Her older-looking boyfriend even tried to get us all into this new movie that we had heard a lot about, but it was rated R for adults, Rocky Horror something something. BTW, we were not able to get in.

After a primer in the bright lights and big city, the day arrived that we were to move out of state. Shit was packed, a van came and took it, our minimally-packed car was gassed up and we headed south on the Northway. I can't even say how long it took us to get there, I vaguely recalled passing by NYC, and then going through New Jersey, but for all intents and purposes the entire trip felt like an off-putting voice-over montage from Taxi Driver.

And then we arrived at the base housing in Virginia, Bethel Manor to be exact.

I didn't go out much when we first got there, I stayed in my room, setting up my stuff in a room that felt foreign. It was a lot of the same stuff I had in New York, but it felt weird here in this cinder-block-walled building. I mowed the lawn, I did chores around the house, etc. I was not particularly interested in going out and discovering Virginia – State Motto: "Virginia is for Lovers," btw – but eventually, Virginia found me.

At some point I had to go get registered at my new high school. The second we walked in, a young lady came up to me and my sister, introduced herself, and proceeded to give us a tour of the school. I met a bunch of other kids who lived in Bethel Manor as well. This school was sort of 50/50 military kids and locals, so there was a pretty good mix. A lot of the local kids were from farm families, so I was used to that already and could communicate with them via the secret language that all farm people know.

The Military Brats – as they were called – were really good at making friends, especially if they had already moved around a lot, so they usually came up to me first and broke the ice. I met a lot of people in the first six months at school, made some friends that I still talk to today. And you know what? Virginia was alright. I really, *really* liked it there, and over the course of the next three years of high school, I carved out a pretty decent rut for myself to settle comfortably into.

Siiiiiiiigggghhhh. So relaxing and predictable, what could ever make me change now? Here's a thought: what about graduation?

Gaaaaaahhhhh!

Why you gotta be that way, anxiety?

IT GOT TO COME OUT

There's a song called *Boogie Chillen* by an ol' Bluesman named John Lee Hooker, and there is a line in that song that states: "It's in him, and it got to come out." I always loved this song, because it embodied what I feel creativity, in general, is like. Even though the song is about a kid who wanted to be a musician, and while I was – and am – not a musician, I look back at the way my life has played out, and the song – and that line – seemed fitting.

For the longest time, I wanted to join the Navy. Very likely because our dad was in the Navy. I also know at one point I wanted to be a forest ranger. You might think this was also due to our father being one, but in point of fact, the lifestyle just really seemed fun and exciting. I loved being outside, I loved camping, hiking and fishing, and I disliked being around people too much.

The ranger thing lasted a long time, like into my twenties, and was only quashed because around that time the rangers were being re-modeled into a sort of Junior State Police, which my father really didn't care much for either at first. But then he was informed that he could carry a bigger gun and arrest people even *more*. Easy sell. Not for me, though.

The "dream," I suppose, for lack of a better word, that lasted longer than the rest, was to do something in the entertainment field. I couldn't narrow it down when I was a kid, mostly because I just had no idea what the scope of "the industry" was, or what it entailed. I liked cartoons, always wanted to do the voices for them, but Mel Blanc had already hogged all of the good gigs for that.

I liked drawing and writing, and was always drawing little cartoon stories or strips. I'd get an idea into my head, and just start going to town creating these comic strip type stories to get the idea out of my head. Like for instance, I saw Planet of the Apes when it first came on TV in the early 70s, and just *loved* it. So I drew my own version of it, painstakingly recreating it scene for scene, but with my own proprietary brand of characters.

My cartoon folks – for reasons I cannot even begin to understand or explain – had human bodies, but hamburger bun heads. So, look at a burger bun sideways, then pinch one side and open the opposite side for the mouth, then slap some round eyes on top – that was my basic human head. I have no earthly idear why I started drawing like that, but there it was.

I did a few stories like this, one was an epic Dungeons & Dragons story that I really got into. We played D&D

every time I visited my mom and her second husband, and mind you this was at the very dawn of the game in the mid 70s. In the Fall of 1977, there was a wargaming convention in Schenectady, and this stepfather, who was really into it, took us for a day.

We got to sit in on a campaign that was DMed by none other than Gary Gygax himself, whom I had no great knowledge about, even though his name was on all the game books. We just so happened to be sitting right next to the table when it was announced that his campaign was starting, so we got signed in quick. It was fun, I loved the concept, I drew the cartoons.

I didn't really realize it back then, but one does not simply draw cartoons, you actually wrote them as well. I just sort of made it up as I went along, but it was writing the story nonetheless. And then it was a natural progression to start writing stories that may have been books had you had any stick-with-it-ness; or, say, actually knew what you were doing. One way or the other, I was now a writer and artist. This would inform my choice of profession later on, and it is something I do to this day.

However, it was in Second Grade, at Mohawk Lake Elementary School, that I had my personal gestalt moment that led me to where I would remain until this day as the thing I wanted to do. I was in a school play; one of those pithy plays where everyone in the class has a part, and there are no auditions, and everyone has at least one line, and there are costumes, and sets made out of cardboard and construction paper, and almost no one plays a human child. It's all clouds and trees and lions and giant pieces of fruit. *That* sort of play.

The performance would take place at the far end of the cafeteria that was designated as The Stage, even though it was not a stage, it was just "that area of the floor." The performances were done in the day time, and parents had to take time off work to attend. I remember so very little on the specifics – except for one thing.

When it came time for me to step forward and deliver my line with the intensity of a young Gielgud or perhaps an Olivier, I suddenly had a revelation or epiphany:

If I said *more* than was scripted, that would be good.

It was sound reasoning, and to this day I have no idea why my teacher would have had any objections in the matter. Directors, go figure. Why can't they just trust the performer's instincts? We know what we're doing.

But also, along with the added dialogue and stage time, I was also able to turn the dramaturgical experience into a somewhat lighter, more fun story, one in which I was the Lead, and it was all about me. It was tough, but I managed; and so convincing and confident was this new play, that I had rewritten on the spot, that the audience was spellbound. They laughed. Then they laughed harder. And those laughs bit me so hard, I was hooked from then on.

I had found my life's work in Grade Two; that was the good news. I lived in the great BFE; that was the bad news.

What was I supposed to do with this newfound passion from here?

Fortunately, classrooms offered a fantastic opportunity for the right performer to hone their craft. The teachers would feed me straight lines, setting them up – and I would knock 'em down with the zingers. It was all so easy, and so appreciated, and appropriate in behavior. The teachers loved it, and they wanted to share me with the fine folks in the school office, where the Principals could enjoy it as well.

Most of my years in school from third to sixth grades, I had my own special seat outside Principal John Blumetti's or Vice Principal Vanderfeld's offices – they passed me back and forth like a pack of cigarettes on D Block. I felt seen.

By 6th grade, someone had suggested I audition for the school play. I heard a great sigh of relief from the direction of the office on the third floor of Pontiac Middle School. I may have heard ol' John Blumetti cry a bit that I would no longer be there that often, now that I was a professional. I'm sorry, John, but I had to follow my destiny.

I loved the plays I did at Pontiac, and surprisingly always got cast as the comic relief, which was fine with me, man, I had enough drama at home and at school as it was. Sixth and Seventh Grade plays had me playing a questionably-moraled real estate salesman and a snarky butler, and left me wanting more.

Somehow, around this time, my father had decided that he wanted to do some acting as well, and he got some great roles in some classic stage musicals such as Guys and Dolls, Camelot, Fiddler on the Roof and whatnot. He had a great singing voice, and that bludgeoning baritone that met us when we broke windows, was also good at reaching the back of the house in the local community theater productions.

He met his second wife in community theater, and on a couple occasions, when there was a Variety-type show, he got me in the cast as well. Ironically enough, my partner in crime would end up being John Blumetti's daughter, who was about my age. We punctuated the song my dad was singing with his new wife, in a literal way, as they crooned Indian Love Call to each other a la Nelson Eddy and Jeanette MacDonald. Nothing but laughs that fed my soul.

When I moved to Virginia with my mom, I for some reason stumbled a bit before getting into theater again. Likely my low self-esteem. I found it a somewhat con-founding, and an aggravating travail, as the handsome football-playing types took the lead roles because they already had a following, bumping the "real" actors down to the supporting roles, and bumping me even lower on occasion. I still managed to get some nice comic roles, and even did a few experimental, Off Off Broadway type shows like A Game and Death Knocks.

By my Senior year, even despite my best efforts to not be labeled, I was voted Class Clown, and it was generally assumed that I would be a huge Hollywood star within a year after graduation. No pressure there, right? A buddy of mine and I did actually have a plan to go to Hollywood in a round-about way after graduation.

My friend had a friend who lived in San Diego, and he was dabbling in the industry, so we had a plan to party our asses off at UVA with some friends before we took the Amtrack to San Diego, to roommate until we could get settled, and kick off our careers as famous stars.

Oh my, the level of ignorance that we had in our back pockets as to how shit worked in life. Through a chain of events I can only describe as cleverly-written plot-twists, I wound up in Las Vegas by myself, living with my mom and stepfather who was now stationed at Nellis AFB.

After licking my wounds, I figured I knew myself well-enough to know I would not have done well on my own in California, and I decided to stay in Vegas, where at the age of 17, I started to do stand-up at local open mics and comedy showcases.

After a few false starts, my first time on stage was at The Continental Hotel and Casino's small musical stage, where a guy named Gary Bruno gave you five minutes to prove yourself, or eliminate yourself. Luckily, I made the cut, and was a staple at that showcase for a few years, providing the yocks in between the musical sets of The Last Band, the house musicians that played a nice mix of blues, soul and rock.

I was 17, which had some issues; such as I was technically too young to be allowed in the stage area or gambling areas, or bar area. The stage was next to gambling machines on one side, and the bar on the other; when I wanted a glass of water I had to go to the bar – where they would ask for my ID.

"For water?" I asked pleasantly.

"Yes," the bartender replied, deadpan.

"For a stupid glass of fucking WATER?" I inquired in my most understanding voice, not being in any way combative. "Are you FUCKING KIDDING ME?"

"SECURITY." The bartender rejoined.

I was escorted out of that casino a few times a week, as more shows were added. Seems the bartender had decided to make me a pet project. So I grew this awesome 17-year-old's beard, which easily made me look older, like I was maybe 18. I took to hiding in the shadows of the stage area, but I would get spotted at some point, and gracefully escorted out one door. Then I would run – and I mean I *literally* ran – around the side and sneak in another door. I don't like to brag too much, but my record for getting tossed out of that joint was four times in one night.

That came to an end when the leader of The Last Band, a cool cat named Art Groom, came to my rescue one night. I was in the middle of a solid perp-walk session courtesy of the 6'6" former Navy Seal named Carl, when I felt a hand on my shoulder. I looked back and saw Art – this 40-year-old lifer musician who was damned near blind in both eyes, was almost as tall as Carl, and spoke in a low, smooth growl.

"It's okay, man" he said, "the kid's with me."

I am pretty damn sure Carl was looking forward to water-boarding me out in the parking lot, but he looked at Art, side-eyed the living shit out of me, and let go of my arm.

"Come on, man, let's go grab a drink," Art said. And we went to the bar, Art nodded to the bartender, and we got a couple beers.

WOW. That was some of the baddest-assed shit I had ever seen. We sat there and talked for quite some time, turns out we both dug the same music, both loved comic books, and both had the same sense of humor.

I think about Art a lot when I think about where I started and where I am now; and I credit him with giving me some of the best advice I had even been given when it comes to the industry, or even just life in general. I never had a great amount of self-esteem when I was kid, and I tended to trust people who I viewed as being authority figures, whether they actually were or not.

As a result of this, I got my ass handed to me a lot by these older, more experienced, jerk-faced asshole "comedians" whose idea of being great comics relied mainly on their ability to tear down other comics right before they went on stage, causing them to have a bad set. Then when the asshole went up, by comparison, they looked better. In theory.

When these guys tore me apart – disguised as "helpful input" – it really got to me. I never talked myself up, in fact I always talked myself down. I never even signed any of the cartoons I drew for The Last Band that Art used as promotional materials, and sent out all over the city and quite a few other states.

One night I was getting torn apart in a passive-aggressive way by this one guy right before I went on. Art walked over and just gave that clown a look, and he backed right away, never bothered me anymore.

After my set, Art sat me down and said:

"There are plenty of folks in life who are going to jump at the chance to dump on you. Don't be the first one in that line."

I thanked him, he downed his brandy, then got up to start his next set, when he suddenly turned back to me

"Sign your damn cartoons."

I never got thrown out of the Continental again. After the comedy showcase folded a few years later, I followed the Last Band everywhere they played, and Art and I stayed friends until he passed away decades later.

Art and I were sitting at a bar during his break one night, when the maudlin, worry-wart 18-year-old inside me took the wheel for a second.

"You ever think about what happens when you stop getting gigs?" I asked him.

He looked up slowly from his Budweiser and Christian Brothers back, turned to me with a bemused look on his face. "That's a dumb fuckin' question, man" he stated, then went back to his own thoughts.

From where I sit now, I see that I would have the same answer for any young person asking me the same question. It simply isn't an option. As long as it's in you, it's got to come out – some way, some how.

Art wound up working until the day he died, playing his Hammond B3 and growling out lyrics. The main stage at the Sand Dollar in Vegas was renamed The Art Groom Stage when he passed.

Seemed fitting.

ABOUT THE AUTHOR

Greg Dorchak's family moved to upstate New York in 1965 when he was a baby. For the next 13 years his playground was the High Peaks Region of the Adirondack Park, 6 million acres of lakes, trees, mountains, and colorful people.

Though he has been gone for over 40 years, the Adirondacks still occupy a big part of his memory and personality. In OF PIGS AND METEORITES, Dorchak recounts some of the memories that made up his formative years, with humor, introspection, a lot of snark, and a little bit of humanity.

* 9 7 9 8 8 6 8 9 1 1 8 2 8 *